The Devil's Deal

PEARSON

At Pearson, we believe in learning – all kinds of learning for all kinds of people. Whether it's at home, in the classroom or in the workplace, learning is the key to improving our life chances.

That's why we're working with leading authors to bring you the latest thinking and the best practices, so you can get better at the things that are important to you. You can learn on the page or on the move, and with content that's always crafted to help you understand quickly and apply what you've learned.

If you want to upgrade your personal skills or accelerate your career, become a more effective leader or more powerful communicator, discover new opportunities or simply find more inspiration, we can help you make progress in your work and life.

Pearson is the world's leading learning company. Our portfolio includes the Financial Times, Penguin, Dorling Kindersley, and our educational business, Pearson International.

Every day our work helps learning flourish, and wherever learning flourishes, so do people.

To learn more please visit us at: www.pearson.com/uk

The Devil's Deal

An insider's tale of how money is made

Andreas Loizou

Harlow, England • London • New York • Boston • San Francisco • Toronto • Sydney • Auckland • Singapore • Hong Kong
Tokyo • Seoul • Taipei • New Delhi • Cape Town • São Paulo • Mexico City • Madrid • Amsterdam • Munich • Paris • Milan

PEARSON EDUCATION LIMITED

Edinburgh Gate
Harlow CM20 2JE
Tel: +44 (0)1279 623623
Fax: +44 (0)1279 431059
Website: www.pearson.com/uk

First published in Great Britain in 2012
© Andreas Loizou 2012

ISBN: 978-0-273-75797-9

British Library Cataloguing-in-Publication Data
A catalogue record for this book is available from the British Library

Library of Congress Cataloging-in-Publication Data
A catalog record for this book is available from the Library of Congress

10 9 8 7 6 5 4 3 2 1
16 15 14 13 12

Typeset in 9pt Stone Serif by 3
Printed and bound by Ashford Colour Press Ltd, Gosport

For Maria and Nicolas, with love and gratitude

Contents

Acknowledgements

Many thanks to Christopher Cudmore for his belief and guidance.

I've had some fantastic teachers along the way. Thanks to Louise Doughty, Midge Gillies, Richard Skinner and John Murray. Special thanks to Mark Billingham for two bits of advice I will never forget. I'm grateful to all at Faber & Faber, especially Patrick Kehoe.

Richard Bastin, as well as being a great friend, was a world-class sounding board. Andrew Zelouf was incredibly generous with his ideas and time. Ouida Taaffe has helped immeasurably, as have Jane Burke and Jo Parry-Gocke.

David Green and David Atkins commented on early versions of this story. Simon Scott and Peter Williams kept my spirits up during difficult times. I apologise to Mark and Lizzie Waugh for ruining their holiday with my graphs and diagrams. Meirion Jones, Jay Rayner, Andy Round and John Tague offered valuable support and encouragement. Anna Jackson, Melanie Carter, Dorothy McCarthy, Gareth Williams, Anne Heaton-Ward and Irene Boston all served with distinction.

Heartfelt thanks are given to the staff of Guy's and Addenbrooke's, without whom there would be neither book nor author.

A final, a huge thank you to Monica and Helena. I'm back with you now.

How it all began

I've got one of the great jobs.

My work takes me to Europe, Asia and the Americas. I've never shaken off my teenage travel bug, so I accept offers from anywhere – Wall Street, Hong Kong, Cairo – as long as a business class flight is part of the deal. I love the role, love talking in front of people, love that moment when the penny drops and they understand.

But a chance meeting with the investment director of a secretive private bank changed my life for ever. Guy Abercrombie had been one of my students and now he was an immensely rich man. How had he become so successful so quickly? What was the knowledge he had and others didn't? He promised to tell me, and that's when my problems began.

If you've ever been intrigued about how bankers make money, then this is the book for you. It will explain the secret techniques and cunning schemes of the money men. It'll tell you more than you ever wanted to know. While writing this book I've continually asked myself this question: how would you benefit from learning what my mysterious client knew?

I've written *The Devil's Deal* with two audiences in mind. I want new visitors to this strange world to understand why we lurch from one financial crisis to another. If you've ever been intrigued by the secret techniques and cunning schemes of the money men, then this is the book for you. Use it as a guidebook to finance, with translations of the most common phrases included for free. Readers already working in banking will enjoy how the truth about the financial world is revealed. You'll recognise some of the characters around your office: you might even recognise yourself.

I've had to change the names of certain characters and firms to avoid even more letters from lawyers. And, in two very important instances, I've been advised to change the location for reasons of personal safety. The people involved are unlikely to complain about being made anonymous.

The Devil's Deal is the ultimate insider's tale. *The Devil's Deal* is also a thriller. And it's true.

one

One-way ticket

chapter

From Zurich to disaster

Day 1, 9.30am – Zurich

Uli isn't the smartest of my former students. But he manages $5 billion of other people's money and I mentor him on how to invest.

Uli's a polite guy. When I've finished our quarterly meetings he normally hands me a present for my nephew Alex. Today, though, Uli is uncharacteristically distracted. Excited, and a little nervous, he tells me he won't be able to drive me down to Zurich station.

'I've got a new client coming this afternoon,' Uli says in his sing-song Swiss-German accent. 'He's got €50 million to invest.'

'Great!' I'm genuinely happy for Uli. Plus I'm already calculating how much I can put up my fees.

'Great!' agrees Uli, but he holds his smile too long and I know that something's wrong. I've been advising Uli for ten years, ever since he was a graduate on a course I led at Goodman Rozel. I can tell when he's worried. He calls his secretary and shakes my hand. 'I've bought something for Alex but you'll need to collect it from the shop.' He hands me a receipt for Christof's Toys and I read an address in the old town. I leave him, stumbling past piles of annual accounts and broker reports which spill across the floor.

Clients like Uli give me an insider's access. I know what will happen to certain companies weeks before the stock market even sniffs a rumour. Part of my job is helping financial experts communicate to 'normal' people. I write their presentations, prepare their speeches to shareholders and coach them on how to deal with the more aggressive financial journalists. My clients trust me with inside information and I've never abused that trust.

It's a well-rewarded job, and I was just thinking how much I still enjoyed learning new things, when the bomb exploded.

Day 1, 11.00am – Zurich Airport

I saw flames and smoke, and the ambulances driving past the crowds. CNN cut to protesters running away from tanks. I read the subtitles flashing across the TV screen – *state of emergency, many civilians feared dead* – and dunked a square of creamy chocolate into my coffee. A groan went round the business lounge at Zurich Airport as they announced all flights were grounded. A fat man next to me muttered a multi-lingual stream of expletives. 'Damn terrorists. Why should we suffer because they've blown up some airport?'

I mumbled something in reply but I was already thinking about how to get a train back to London. As was everyone else in the lounge.

I took a taxi to the old town and walked towards Bahnhofstrasse. Underneath all these private banks lie the great vaults. Miles and miles of gold and silver, diamonds and platinum. I walked over cellars stuffed with loot from Latin American drug lords and stolen development funds snatched by African warlords. Who knew who owned it all?

Day 1, 11.30am – Paradeplatz, Zurich

I managed to book a seat on the 12.30pm train to Paris. Not ideal, of course, but at least it would get me closer to home. I was desperate to get back: I was delivering a course in New York in three days' time and needed to prepare. With an hour to spare I headed over to pick up the model train. I was hit by a warm gust of Havana cigar smoke. The man I presumed to be Christof scrunched a jeweller's magnifying optic into his right eye to look at Uli's receipt. Short and stocky like most men of Zurich, he reminded me a little of Uli.

'The Mountain Express Train.' Christof handed me the latest addition to Alex's ever-growing model rail collection. 'It's already gift-wrapped.' The train felt reassuringly heavy in my hands.

Zurich was a model village of order and calm. I took in the town hall clock, the steeples of the churches, the trams gliding over the glistening rails. But in the train queue I had that weird feeling when someone you don't remember recognises you. Who was the young man who looked me in the eye as two porters fussed over his luggage and ushered him into First Class?

I've taught a lot of people over the years. Investment bankers in Malaysia, bond traders in Mexico City, people I now suspect are money-launderers in Marbella. Thousands of students, from interns to managing directors, have had the unalloyed joy of watching me in action. Being a trainer is a bit like being a prefect at school: all the younger kids know your name and remember what you look like but there are loads of people you can't recall.

But as we pulled out of Zurich station I was puzzled. I was sure I'd seen the man before and, what's more, I'm sure he knew me. Where was it? It was irritating, like having a favourite song playing in your mind and not being able to recall the title or the singer.

The hefty chap who had mumbled to me at the airport was now slumped next to my seat. I sank into a roll of his flesh hanging over my side of the armrest. He huffed himself towards the window, clearing me three extra centimetres of body room for the remaining seven hours of the journey.

The guard checked the man's passport against his ticket. 'I hope you enjoy the journey, Mr Conrad.'

'How can I? We are sure to be late.'

I did my best to avoid eye-contact. In my briefcase was a small pile of reports I'd taken from Uli's swamped offices. They were the usual stuff – flimsy broker notes solely designed to drive commissions from clients – but my eyes were drawn to a more substantial analyst report. Cal-Pan was a Hong Kong-registered company. It ran a number of huge infrastructure projects, most of which relied on government funding. Strange, but I couldn't remember putting the report in my case.

The analyst believed that the shares were a strong buy. But she wouldn't be the first stock-picker to get things badly wrong ...

case study

Analyse this – Henry Blodget

The job of an equity analyst is to tell clients if a share should be bought or sold. Henry Blodget became a symbol for all that was rotten about the trade.

Blodget first came to fame (and that's not too strong a word for what happened) when he predicted a massive rise in the price of a smart new e-retailer called Amazon. The stock rose 128 per cent and soon Blodget was the number-one-rated internet expert in the world. Blodget's stock picks made tons of money for his investors and his every pronouncement was hungrily devoured by his acolytes.

A high-profile job at Merrill Lynch came with a massive salary and an obligation to recommend many internet shares as Strong Buys. (See Chapter 3 for more on buy and sell recommendations.) At the same time, however, Blodget was calling their shares *crap, junk* and *pieces of shit* in his personal emails.

Easy money blinded everyone to the massive conflicts of interest. Everyone, that is, except for Eliot Spitzer, attorney general and governor of New York. Blodget was charged with securities fraud by the SEC (Securities and Exchange Commission) and paid a $2 million fine and had to return a further $2 million of his ill-gotten gains. He agreed to a ban from working in the securities industry.

Blodget lost $700,000 of his own money on internet donkeys he'd selected for his personal portfolio. He is now a huge fan of passive investing (see Chapter 19 for more on this subject). This approach rejects highly-paid analysts in favour of a long-term *buy and hold* strategy. I wonder if the loss had anything to do with his change of mind?

I levered myself up from the seat and walked to the front of the carriage where they kept a stack of newspapers and business magazines. It was going to be a long, long journey and I was determined to have enough reading material to get through it.

Sitting down across from my portly co-traveller was a beautiful woman. She was so different from Conrad that she might have come from a separate biological species. She pushed her North Face holdall into the luggage rack. Big and red, it stood out like a bloodstain amongst the beige and grey luggage spilling from the racks. I read her name tag – Anisa Chabbra – and saw a home address in South London. Splayed open on the table in front of her was a book I recognised from a long way back. It's called *Emotional Investment: What Your Bank Account Says About Your Love Life!*

The rules of compounding

Conrad was explaining to Anisa Chabbra how compounding worked.

❝ Compounding is the most powerful technique in finance ❞

'Compounding is the most powerful technique in finance. And also one of the simplest to understand.' He talked her through the first example in *Emotional Investment*. 'Imagine you hand over your savings to a bank. You agree an interest rate for a year. At the end of the year, if you don't take out your interest, your money will grow.'

On 1 January 2012 you deposit money in a bank	$1,000
The bank pays interest for a year at the rate of	4%
So, you get this much money for the year	$40
(That's $1,000 multiplied by 4%)	
Which means at the end of 2012 your money has grown to	$1,040
(Your original $1,000 plus the $40 of interest)	

'The value of compounding is affected by two things – the interest rate you get, and the length of time you can leave your money in the bank. Let's see what happens to your investment if you leave your money with the bank for another two years.'

2013	
Opening amount	$1,040.00
Interest at 4%	$41.60
Closing amount	$1,081.60

2014	
Opening amount	$1,081.60
Interest at 4%	$43.26
Closing amount	$1,124.86

'In the second year you'll earn interest on both your original capital and the interest from the first year. And in the third year, the interest on the interest grows even more. It's like a snowball rolling down a gentle hill. You put your money in a bank, then just sit back and watch your nest egg grow.'

I had to concede that Conrad knew the basics, even if his metaphors were a little scrambled. But only a fool believes banks are risk-free these days.

---

fast facts

Three facts about compound interest ...

Start as **early** as you can. This is a long-term strategy, not a get-rich-quick scheme.

Be prepared to **move your money** to find the best interest rates.

Small differences in costs and **fees** can **have a huge impact** in the long term. You have been warned.

And an opinion and a myth about compound interest:

Don't become a miser. **Fun today** is also a good way to live your life.

Loads of websites claim Albert Einstein called compound interest **the greatest mathematical discovery of all time**. He didn't, but why let the truth get in the way of a good story?

Whatever you want

Anisa Chabbra picked up her book. 'It says here that everyone needs a financial expert to help them invest.'

'No. Investment is much simpler than that. There are basically only two types of investor. Once you understand what they want, then you understand money. Throw away that silly book, and I'll tell you what I've learned about money in my many years of investment.'

'What are the two types?' Anisa had obviously decided that Conrad was a harmless old windbag. And she was probably desperate to have a distraction for the long journey.

'I'm the first type, my dear. I'm older and I try as hard as I can to preserve my capital. I'll do anything to avoid risk. I need my investments to give me a regular income because I'm retired and I don't have a job. My investments need to give dividends or interest.'

'What's a dividend?'

'A dividend is a payment made by a company to shareholders out of its profit for the year.'

'OK,' she said.

'What would you rather have – a company that paid you a big dividend every year or a company that paid you nothing?'

Anisa rushed her answer. 'A company that paid me something every year.'

'No. You have to consider the question a little more carefully, young lady. What would happen if the company paid *all* of its profits out every year?'

Conrad's condescending tone was already irritating me. I wondered what effect it was having on poor Anisa Chabbra. I decided to be the gallant knight and chip in. 'It can't re-invest the profits and so it won't be able to grow.' Anisa smiled at me, a great big red-lipstick grin that said we were on the same side now.

Conrad continued, a little irritated at me interrupting his flow. 'It can't buy a new factory or take over a competitor or research new products. Or employ more staff.'

'Or launch a high-quality – and very expensive – training programme to get the best possible value out of its new recruits.'

I smiled, but Conrad carried on as if I'd said nothing. 'If the company pays out loads of dividends, it might be great because you've got all the money in your hands. But the problem is that the company has no money left to plough back into growth. Ask yourself again: what would you prefer?'

'OK, this time I'll choose a company that keeps all of its money.'

I took up the theme. I was aware that I was sounding a little bit like a teacher, but that's an occupational hazard. 'Shares make more sense for someone your age, Anisa. You buy a share, and the idea is over the next twenty years the company reinvests the money and grows. If all goes well, the share price goes up and you can sell it. Then you'll be able to live off your capital gains.'

Gains and losses

Many people buy shares for capital gains

'Because the price of shares is volatile, you need to be able to calculate your return in per cent. Look, here's a share I bought which had a fantastic year and I made a big capital gain.'

On 1 January 2011 I bought a share for	£10
And on 31 December it's worth	£16
My capital gain for the year is	£6
In percentage terms I made	60%
(which is the gain of £6 divided by the original value of £10)	

But every rose has its thorn

Conrad snatched the paper from me. 'But, my friend, you haven't mentioned just how easily your share could have plummeted in value.' Conrad had the gift of making the word 'friend' sound like a threat. 'Here's my calculation of what could have happened if the share fell in price and you made a capital loss.'

On 1 January 2011 you bought a share for	£10
But on 31 December it's worth	£6
Your capital loss for the year is	−£4
In percentage terms you've lost	−40%
(which is the loss of £4 divided by the original value of £10)	

'You are one of nature's pessimists, Mr Conrad.'

'Pah!' Conrad spat out. 'Long-term investments wouldn't work for me. I can't wait around for the promise of future returns. In twenty years' time I won't be here.'

The train screeched to a halt. We still hadn't made it as far as Basel.

'Don't be too sure about that,' I said.

---

fast facts

What sort of person prefers steady income to capital gain?

They are probably old ... and they'll be reliant on their savings. They probably haven't got a job, so they need income from their investments.

... and are not able to take many risks. You've got to be more of a risk-taker to buy shares for capital gain. If you're after the upside, you've got to be able to cope with the downside.

They rely on the investment for income ... This may be their only source of current income. No one likes to lose money, but for some people it could be fatal.

... and their cultural background is one which values stability. You may have been brought up by entrepreneurs who spent their leisure time gambling at casinos or at the race track. Or you may be the child of civil servants who worked in the same office for forty years. Upbringing has a huge impact on every choice we make.

They may be investing for the benefit of others. There's a huge difference between trying to make a quick buck to pay for a flashier car, or investing for your grandchildren's education.

We didn't move for twenty minutes. Delays on the Swiss railway system are extremely rare and I couldn't see why we were stalled. I was beginning to get irritated when I felt a tap on my shoulder. It was the man from the queue.

'Hello. You may not remember me ...'

I said: 'To be honest, I recognise you but sorry, I can't place you.'

'Don't worry.' Abercrombie's smile was disarming. 'You must get this all the time. Ten years ago you taught me when I was a graduate at Goodman Rozel.' The conductor announced our departure in German, French, Italian and English. 'My name is Guy Abercrombie. You told me everything I needed to make money.'

I laughed. 'So the course was successful?'

'Yes. Very, very successful.'

I said, 'How successful?'

'Millions and millions of pounds successful.'

'I reckon you owe me lunch.'

Day 1, 1.30pm – The dining carriage of the Zurich to Paris train

We sat in the pristine dining carriage. My salmon terrine hadn't even arrived when Abercrombie leant forward. 'Shall I tell you how I did it?'

'Go on.'

The immaculately-suited waiters served our starters. Guy began to tell me what he was doing at work and I was gobsmacked. Absolutely astounded.

'Is this all true?' I asked him.

'Every word.' Abercrombie's phone vibrated and he snatched it up from the table. He listened intently and whispered two words. 'Buy oil.' He turned back to me. 'I have to go back to my carriage to make some calls. I'll come down and find you as soon as I can. And then I'll tell you exactly what I've got planned.'

2

Taking risks

Day 1, 3.00pm – My carriage on the Zurich to Paris train

Back in economy Conrad was still lecturing poor Anisa. 'An investor is someone who has surplus cash and wants to use it to make even more money.'

'Or someone who can't find anything they want to spend their money on now!'

I had to laugh at her cheek. I decided to make Anisa my pupil. 'True. Investment is really about delaying your spend. Investors postpone parting with their cash. You could leave your money in a bank but, to be honest, that's a little bit of a stupid thing to do. You'll get very, very little in return. Do you ever look at those tiny numbers at the bottom of your bank statement? They are the insulting amounts the bank gives you if you are in credit.'

❝ Investment is really about delaying your spend ❞

'What do you advise?'

'It's better to buy an investment asset. These come in different shapes and sizes. It all depends on the risk of the investment.'

Anisa said, 'I was just reading about risk in *Emotional Investment*.'

'What does it tell you?'

'It seems that men are very different from women when it comes to choosing investments. Especially when it comes to commitment.

And,' Anisa continued, 'it seems the word *risk* doesn't automatically mean something bad for you financial gurus.'

'That's right. For you, risk always means something bad. There's the risk of breaking your leg skiing, or the risk of losing your job. By the way, where is it you said you work?'

'I didn't.' Anisa smiled at me again but this time her eyes remained cold. She wasn't a woman who gave too much away about herself. Never mind, I told myself, plenty of time left to find out more about her.

I continued. 'Money men don't see risk in the same way as the general public. In fact, we love risk. Risk leads to return. And return is our objective.'

Take a chance on me

'I'll give you an example. The safest investment in any country is normally a government bond. Let's assume you buy a Japanese government bond which pays 3 per cent every year. You plan to hold it for ten years, so your money can compound.

'But if you took some risk, you could get a lot more return. How much would you get in ten years if you chose an investment which paid 10 per cent per year? And what about 20 per cent?'

Anisa invests ¥100,000 for 10 years
At 3%, her money will grow to   ¥134,392
At 10%, her money will grow to   ¥259,374
At 20%, her money will grow to   ¥619,174

Conrad put up a pudgy hand to interrupt. 'But risk means that you can lose all your money. Why gamble with your savings? When I receive money from my associates I want to preserve my capital and get some growth. And I want to do it without taking any risk.'

Inflation has a big effect on your real return

'But you've forgotten one really big thing, Mr Conrad. *Inflation.* Inflation eats away at your returns. Bank adverts always quote the *nominal return* but what's vital to us is the *real return*. This is what you get once you've stripped out the pernicious impact of inflation. The lower your headline return, the bigger the hit from inflation. Inflation causes money to lose its purchasing power.'

I sketched these figures out on a napkin.

If the nominal rate of Return is …	3%
… you need to strip out inflation of	2%
… to find the real rate of return	1%

Conrad looked crestfallen. Some men can turn anything into a competition. He was clearly determined to have the last word on this subject.

'You young people think I'm some sort of fuddy-duddy. But I've made steady returns over many years just by picking low-risk investments.' Conrad gave me the smile of a fat cat who owned a fund dealing solely in premium-rated cream. 'You can think of me as the poor man's Warren Buffett.'

'Who?' asked Anisa.

---

case study

Who's Warren Buffett?

He's the best investor the world has ever seen, that's all.

Buffett is the living embodiment of the *value investor*. He buys shares when he believes them to be *undervalued* and because they have *long-term* potential ('our favourite holding period is forever'). He prefers simple businesses that produce a *long stream*

▶ *of cash flow.* The next time you buy a pack of four Gillette razor blades for £10, stop for a second and consider how much of that is pure profit for Gillette's shareholders.

Buffett's got a sense of humour, too, something which is not always shared with the stuffed shirts of Wall Street: 'Rule No. 1: Never lose money. Rule No. 2: Never forget Rule No. 1.'

Buffett has spent the last decade at the top of the world's rich lists, but is personally frugal and has vowed to donate 99 per cent of his wealth to charity. His annual letters to shareholders and TV appearances are masterpieces of self-deprecating humour. But behind this folksy exterior is one of global finance's smartest operators: 'Of the billionaires I have known, money just brings out the basic traits in them. If they were jerks before they had money, they are simply jerks with a billion dollars.'

It takes a special kind of billionaire – humble, stable, acutely self-aware of how he is perceived – to get away with that sort of joke. And you have to admire a man who has condemned the wasteful way companies are run, and then buys a corporate jet with Berkshire Hathaway's money. Calling the plane *The Indefensible* makes the joke even funnier.

So that's Buffett, and we got through that without using his nickname, *The Sage of Omaha.*

Weird fact – there are at least fifty books currently available which have Buffett's name in the title. The only living person with more on the shelves is the Dalai Lama, whose investment strategies are unrecorded.

Switzerland is the most beautiful country in which I've led courses. We passed shimmering lakes and snow-capped mountains. Trust Conrad to ruin the mood: 'We are sure to be late. The police will triple-check every passport because of these insurrections in the Middle East.'

We stopped at Strasbourg and Conrad puffed out some hot air and closed his eyes. Anisa picked up her book but looked at me. 'I don't really understand.'

The business of risk

I made a list of four possible investments on the inside cover of *Emotional Investment.*

Shares in a supermarket
Government bond in your country
Shares in a Russian oil company
Shares in a luxury holiday company

'You have to know all the risks before you buy any investment. Which one do you reckon is the safest?'

'The government bond. But I'm not really sure why.'

A bond is an IOU

'A bond is a contract between the government (which is short of funds) and a lender (who's looking for somewhere to invest). Unless the country goes bust, your money will be safe. When you read textbooks on government bonds, they always say governments never default on their payments of interest or the repayment of capital. That's simply not true any more. But government bonds should still be the safest investment you can buy in a country. A government relies on tax income – personal income tax, taxes on the profits of companies, sales taxes and many, many more – to pay back the lender. Or, the government can borrow even more money to pay off its loans.'

Anisa nodded, so I continued. 'So, let's put the bond at the top of the list and then look at our three other choices.'

Government bond in your country	Safest
2	Low risk
3	Medium risk
4	High risk

'Hold on,' she said. 'I'm not sure of the differences between a bond and a share.'*

'The income on a bond is guaranteed. If the company goes bust, the bond holder is towards the front of the queue of people who will be paid. An investor's time exposure to a bond is known in advance. An investor planning a specific event in their life – paying a child's university fees, for example – will have more control.'

'At the end of a bond's life, the borrower has to return the principal, which is the borrowed money. And bonds tend to have a very liquid market, so if an investor needs cash their bond can normally be sold quickly.'

Shares can be low risk, medium risk and high risk

'When you buy shares, you take the risks that the price may fall and the dividend may not be paid. Unlike the government bond, future price movements and dividends from a share are uncertain.'

'When you analyse shares you have to be aware of *company-specific risks*. These risks are unique to an individual company.'

---

fast facts

Five ways to create company-specific risk

Create an environmental disaster, and delay your response. The clean-up after the Gulf of Mexico spill will cost BP at least $20 billion.

---

* The words *share*, *equity* and *common stock* are pretty much interchangeable in the financial markets. We will cover the differences between bonds and shares in more detail in Chapters 5 and 6.

Rely on a fantasist for the majority of your profits, and make sure no one controls him. Nick Leeson's unsupervised trading in derivatives reduced the value of Barings, Britain's oldest and stuffiest merchant bank, to a single, solitary pound.

Get left behind with your technology, and then think everybody else has got it wrong. Hands up if you thought that iPhones, BlackBerrys and Androids were not going to take over the world. That's what Nokia believed, and they lost their pre-eminent global position in mobiles as a result.

Make faulty products, and try to hide their defects. Selling cars that go faster when you press on the brake pedal can never be a viable long-term strategy. Toyota's reported refusal to come clean led to hundreds of liability suits in the US, a country not known for low legal costs.

Keep your customers in the dark, and hope they don't notice. Coca-Cola's launch of the British version of Dasani, its bottled water, was a disaster. The water was marketed as being wonderfully pure, but the customers were dismayed to learn that its source was a tap in Sidcup, a suburb of London not synonymous with natural springs. Bad publicity meant that Coca-Cola canned the product's launch across Europe.

'You've got three different shares. Which of the three companies is the safest? Is it the supermarket, the luxury holiday company, or Russian oil?'

The luxury gap

Staple products make for safer shares

'The supermarket,' said Anisa.

'Why?'

'The products it sells are day-to-day essentials. Sales of staple products like bread or toilet roll don't vary much with the economic climate. People will drink the same quantity of tea whether the stock market is up or down.'

'You're right,' I said. 'Sales are always going to be pretty steady, whatever happens to variables such as inflation, unemployment or the yield to maturity on a forty-year Tibetan government zero bond.'

Government bond in your country	Safest
Shares in a supermarket	Low risk
3	Medium risk
4	High risk

'That leaves us with luxury holidays or Russian oil. What's it to be?'

Anisa delayed her response. 'Both of them seem risky to me. To be honest, I can't decide between them.'

Luxuries make for more risky shares

'There are two factors which drive luxuries. The first is the economy and the second is the strength of the brand.'

'Let's start with what's happening in the economy. Are we enjoying a massive boom or are we stuck in a deep recession? Imagine this bank has a fantastic year and decides to pay you a mega-bonus. What are you going to spend it on? Luxury holidays, or more cornflakes from the supermarket?'

'I'm obviously going to spend more on luxuries,' Anisa said. 'But my consumption of staple goods will stay pretty much the same. During a boom the luxury holiday company is going to have great sales.'

'That's right. A 2 per cent increase in economic activity might lead to a 20 per cent increase in sales. Sadly the opposite is also true. If economic activity falls by 2 per cent, sales of luxury goods may drop by 20 per cent. But a supermarket remains relatively unaffected by the economic climate. It may sell more lobster and profiteroles during a boom, and more white sliced bread and baked beans during a recession, but core sales will stay the same.'

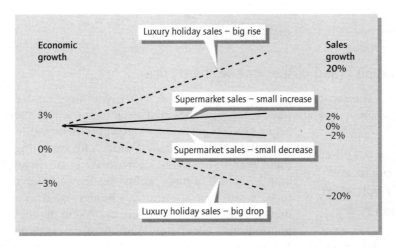

'Luxury goods – expensive holidays, smart cars, branded clothing – represent discretionary spending. They are not essential. You only buy them when you're feeling wealthy and confident about the future.' (We'll go deeper into slumps and booms in Chapters 20–22.)

'But what about the super-rich?' she asked. 'Aren't they insulated from swings in the economy?'

'Yes. David Beckham won't cut back on his Armani because of a rise in unemployment. But many customers will, and these are the people who make most of the money for the luxury goods companies. If the economy is booming, you might well be happy to buy a pair of Jimmy Choo sandals for $400. But if you're scared about finding your rent that month, you'll probably keep your old ones or buy a cheaper brand. And that's why a lot of luxury goods companies lose their appeal for investors when the economy is going bad.'

Government bond in your country	Safest
Shares in a supermarket	Low risk
Shares in a luxury holiday company	Medium risk
4	High risk

A strong brand pushes up the share price

'The second major risk factor is brand. When you buy branded goods you are paying for an image that is as important as the actual product or service. Companies spend significant sums inventing, creating and nurturing their brand. Investors know that a successful brand will lead to huge profits. But they also have to be aware that a brand can be destroyed in a matter of seconds. A company can spend decades building up a reputation among customers, only for stupidity, dishonesty or sheer bad luck to destroy it in seconds.'

> **❝ a brand can be destroyed in a matter of seconds ❞**

---

case study

Five destroyed brands

Here are some great examples of how to get it wrong.

Arthur Andersen

The supposedly independent and honest accountants shredded papers which incriminated them in fraud at corruption-ridden energy giant, Enron. When the news leaked out, Andersen's reputation collapsed and clients scrambled to move competitors. In less than a week, the Big Five group of accountants became the Big Four.

Atkins Nutritionals

What could go wrong with a diet that advised you to eat sausages, fat, steak and more sausages? How about the death of its 117kg inventor from congestive heart failure? Atkins filed for bankruptcy in 2005 and, thankfully, has been rescued, so I can make a joke about it being relaunched in a slimmed-down form.

Boo.Com

These style-leaders of the first dot-com wave did build a successful – if short-lived – brand. Sadly, they also burned through £125 million to set up a website that no one could use. Famous for flying junior staff first class to meetings, the company collapsed with debts of £178 million against assets of £1.4 million.

Ratner's Jewellery

Gerald Ratner worked hard to build up his family business until the annual turnover touched £110 million. The next day he made a few jokes about his products, including this zinger: 'People say, "How can you sell this for such a low price?" I say, "Because it's total crap".'

His whip-sharp humour wasn't appreciated by his customers, who stayed away from his shop in droves. Within weeks, the company's market capitalisation had dropped by £500 million and the phrase 'doing a Ratner' became British slang for corporate stupidity.

Satyam

Ramalinga Raju, the founder and chairman of this Indian IT outsourcing firm, resigned after disclosing that he had massively inflated the company's profits for many years. Shares fell 80 per cent as Raju confessed that $1 billion of cash recorded on Satyam's balance sheet was fictitious.

One interesting side-effect of the Satyam scandal was that the contagion spread to the Indian stock market. The Bombay Stock Exchange Index fell by 7.3 per cent as the entire country's reputation was damaged. Investors were afraid other firms in India would reveal similar frauds.

Unfortunate fact – three months before the scandal broke, Satyam received the Golden Peacock award for excellence in corporate governance.

Politics, currency and demand are amongst the risk factors

'The Russian oil company sounds incredibly risky.'

'True. The big risk is political. A new government could come in and nationalise the company you've bought. But think about the product. All businesses need energy. And ask yourself, where is the oil sold?'

'Oil is sold all across the world.'

'And in what currency?'

'Dollars.'

'Correct. We all know that the rouble is risky but the sales of this company are all received in the most popular currency in the world.' (Chapter 14 will teach you more about currency.) 'Selling in dollars is great news for the investor because it will provide some more stability.

'I reckon you've got a very steady demand for the product for many years to come, before a new technology takes over. But it's still by far the riskiest investment in our sample, so we have to rank it last.'

Government bond in your country	Safest
Shares in a supermarket	Low risk
Shares in a luxury holiday company	Medium risk
Shares in a Russian oil company	High risk

Day 1, 4.30pm – The German–French border

Anisa bought me a coffee from the trolley. An Apple iPhone and a Moleskine notebook peeked out from her half-opened Mulberry bag. She wore Nike trainers and Diesel jeans. Even her great big holdall had a label. Brands are so vital for companies and investors, so much more important than food and energy.

I returned to the mysterious research report on Cal-Pan. Was it accident or design that Uli had given it to me when I left Zurich? The analyst recommended the shares as a very strong buy. The company had a near-monopoly in a vital transport link. It was strong in emerging markets and had the backing of numerous governments. Earnings were forecast to grow massively over the next decade and the shares were incredibly underpriced.

We'd stopped at a small country station only ten minutes away from Strasbourg. Two men in dark suits stood together on the solitary platform. The passenger doors didn't open but I saw the men climb into the driver's cabin.

3

The leap of faith

Day 1, 4.45pm – The German–French border

'People who invest for themselves – it could be your parents or you in a few years' time – only consider the return on an investment. That's how much they've made or, sadly, how much they've lost. But professional investors approach this in a totally different way. If you work as a trader or a fund manager you begin with an assessment of the risk and then factor in the return.'

> **begin with an assessment of the risk and then factor in the return**

Safety and danger

I flipped open Anisa's notebook and began drawing a rough graph.

'We start with two lines. The one that goes from left to right indicates the risk of an investment. The further to the right, the more risk you're taking.'

Anisa nodded comprehension.

'And this vertical line is where we put the percentage returns we expect.'

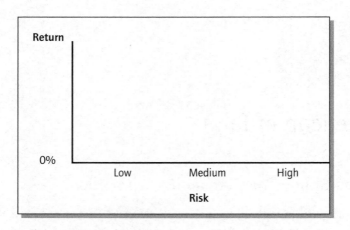

Most government bonds are low risk

'We're now going to plot our investments on this graph. The safest investment is the government bond. What's the risk?'

'Low risk,' she said.

'We've said it's risk-free, and that's why it's as far to the left as it can be. How much return would you expect for a year?'

'No idea.'

'Come on, give me a number between three and five.'

She looked at me with a bemused smile. 'Four.'

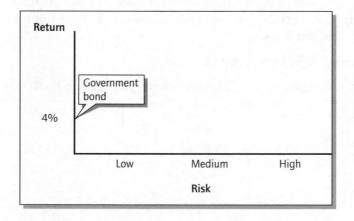

'Good. So the government bond is risk-free and should pay us 4 per cent interest per annum. This is the safest possible investment we can choose. Our capital is pretty much guaranteed. The trade-off is that we will only make a small return. But, remember, some investors are more interested in capital preservation and a regular income than the chance of sky-high gains.'

You demand extra return for moving from bonds to shares

I turned back to my graph. 'Imagine you are the supermarket. How much more return do you need to offer investors? You have to give them some extra reward for moving from the absolute safety of the bond. The supermarket is a relatively safe business, but there are many more risks than with the government bond. How much more return would you need to buy a share in the supermarket?'

Anisa pondered. 'Six per cent more?'

'That means you're looking – on average – for an annual return of 10 per cent from a stable share.'

'Correct. Why don't you plot it on the graph?'

I did.

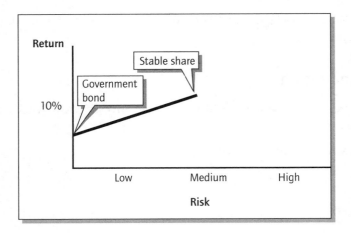

Riskier shares should offer more return

'What about our luxury holiday company?'

'It's medium to high risk,' she said. 'Above the stable equity but below the Russian oil company. I'd take a punt at 15 per cent return every year. I reckon that will cover me for the extra fluctuations in the share price.'

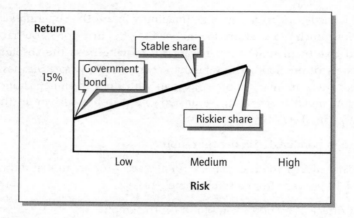

'Your last choice is the Russian oil company. We all know that's super-risky, but if the return is high enough you'll take a chance and invest.'

'It's very risky,' she said. 'I'd need to get 25 per cent return every year.'

Risk and return

I drew a line which linked up the four investments. 'What do you see?'

'Risk and return are linked.'

'And that's the most important lesson you'll ever learn about investment decision-making. If you buy something that's risky, you should be compensated by the possibility of higher rewards. But remember, it's only the possibility.'

'What does this mean in real life?'

'If you want to make loads of money, you've got to be prepared to risk losing your investment. But if safety is your main objective, you'll choose low-risk investments and have to accept a low return.'

'I see. Nothing ventured, nothing gained.'

'That's right. Risk and return are correlated. If you can't afford to lose your capital, you'll choose the government bond and avoid the riskier end of the market. If you can live with the idea of losing your money, then you go in search of higher gains.'

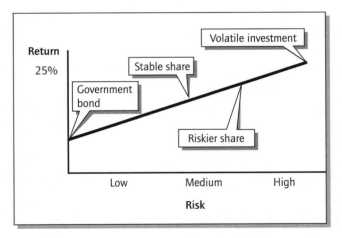

Conrad opened an eye. 'I would never invest in Russia. I'm too cautious. I'd hate to lose all my money in some mad speculation. I couldn't sleep at night.'

'But what about if the share offered 30 per cent?'

'I still wouldn't be interested. I want a steady income and I want my money to be safe. I would rather miss out on a capital gain if it exposed me to the risk of a capital loss.'

'Forty per cent?'

'You're getting warmer.'

'Fifty per cent return per annum? Surely it would be worth the risk?'

Conrad shook his head. 'OK,' he said, but he didn't sound too convinced.

Day 1, 5.30pm – The French countryside

The sun was setting. Anisa yawned and there was a snarl on Conrad's face. 'I think you made a classic mistake when you were talking about risk earlier.'

'What's that?' I asked.

'You've tried to quantify risk. But risk isn't an exact science. Risk in finance means something you didn't expect. And that must include risks you've never even thought of, and have completely ignored because you thought there was no chance of them happening. Look at all the big brains there are in the investment world, and look at all the mistakes they've made.'

Conrad took a sip of coffee before he continued. 'Consider the last financial crisis. According to the experts it should never have happened. But it did. Just because statistics say an event is unlikely, doesn't mean it's never going to happen. The world is full of things that are improbable, but come to pass.'

'Like what?' asked Anisa, slowly stretching herself awake.

'Like this train getting us to Paris.'

'I was thinking more of a business example.'

'Have you ever heard about the sad case of Jérôme Kerviel? He was someone who was badly caught out because his assessment of risk was wrong.'

Jérôme Kerviel – hero and villain

Kerviel lost €4.9 billion trading for the French bank, Société Générale. His strategy was to buy shares, either directly or through derivatives (Chapter 11 will expand your knowledge of derivatives). His investments initially made great returns but the market turned against him and the losses began to mount up.

Critics of Soc Gen say it was impossible for the bank not to know about the trades. There were cries that Kerviel had been made a scapegoat to divert attention from the bank's weak controls and poor management. Kerviel had very limited authority to trade and it's strange that he could do such huge damage in total secrecy. By no means a star at work, the most interesting thing anyone had to say about the small-town boy from Brittany was that he was *unremarkable* or *just like anybody else.*

In court, Kerviel was described as taking risks that were *inhuman* and *stratospheric.* He counter-claimed that Soc Gen turned a blind eye to his trades as they were initially profitable. Kerviel depicts himself in his book, *Caught in the System*, as a financial crusader and a victim of social elitism. He became something of a folk-hero amongst lower-paid employees in the financial world. Presumably, they are all eagerly waiting for the movie which is planned.

What's clear is that Kerviel had no idea of how risk works. If his trades had really been low-risk, it would have been impossible for him to either make or lose large sums. The fact that he made large gains should have alerted him to the possibility of big losses.

During his trial, a fellow trader attempted this analogy. *It's as if Jérôme Kerviel had a mandate to buy 10 tons of strawberries but bought 100 tons of potatoes and the supervisor passes through the hangar every day and says nothing.* With that sort of clarity and logic in the dealing room, it's no wonder that Soc Gen had problems.

Weird fact – Kerviel was sentenced to five years in prison and was also ordered to pay back the €4.9 billion. On release, he hopes to return to his old job in IT. That paid €2,300 per month, so the aloof and brooding Frenchman will need to keep working until he is 177,569 years old to pay back his losses. If he takes no holidays, that is.

Buys and sells

Outside the sky darkened. The mysterious Mr Conrad had fallen silent but Anisa was still full of questions. 'What does it mean when investments don't plot on the expected line of risk and return?'

'Look at the graph now. I've got Investment A and Investment B. Neither of them can be plotted on the line of correlation. How are they different and what is the message they send to investors?'

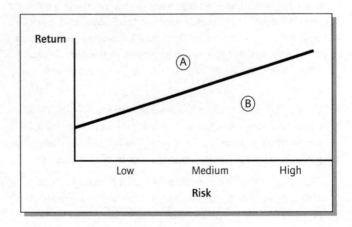

Attractive investments are found above the line

Anisa correctly rated Investment A as a strong buy. 'I'd fill my boots with it!' she announced, to Conrad's amusement.

'Investment A is above the line. For a given level of risk, it's giving investors more return than they'd expect. You've got to buy it!'

I nodded at her to carry on.

'If you buy Investment A before other investors do and they follow you, their purchase orders will push the price of the investment up until risk and return are aligned again. You capture that price rise if you do good analysis, act early and convince the market to follow you. If everything works, there's your capital gain.'

Anisa's explanation was perfect, so I drew the two dotted lines in her notebook.

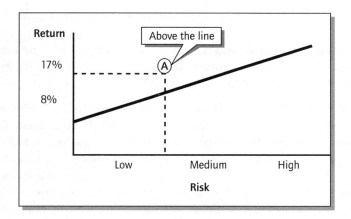

'You can see that most low/medium risk investments will give you about 7 per cent return per year. But Investment A, which has the same low/medium level of risk, is giving you 17 per cent. Any investment which plots above the line is giving us more return than the risk deserves. And that makes Investment A such a clear buy.'

Investments below the line are to be avoided

'Now, take a look at Investment B. Anisa, what do you reckon?'

'It's higher risk, but investors aren't getting the return they deserve.'

'Correct.' I drew the two dotted lines on the flipchart.

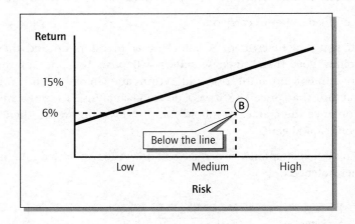

'Investment B is medium/high risk, so investors look for a return about 15 per cent per annum. But the return is a paltry 6 per cent. They should sell any investment below the line.

'Bear in mind that investors can make money out of selling investments as well as buying them. If they sell Investment B before other people, and then other people follow them, then the price will fall. What smart investors do now is buy back the investment and return it to their portfolio. They have the same investment but they've bought it at a lower price. So, they've made money – or at least saved money – by the fall in price.

'A word of warning before you rush to set up your own private trading floors. Both these approaches will only work when two conditions are met. First, your analysis must be correct and, second, enough people must follow you. The investment world is littered with people who've done analysis which has been too obscure, too complicated or too unpopular to be accepted by the rest of the market. Or just wrong.'

Anisa asked a smart question. 'What examples can you give of Investment A and Investment B? I'm looking to make some fast bucks when I get back to London!'

'The sad fact is that investments don't stay as A and B for long. So, by necessity, my examples come from history.'

Many privatisations were above the line

'Most government sell-offs are above the line.' (We'll look at similar deals in more detail when I tell you about Jerry Witts.) 'The companies are normally well-established, with many existing clients and very little competition. They are in steady, dependable industries: electricity production, for example, or water and gas. And governments are often very eager to raise money quickly, so the shares tend to be below their true values when the company is privatised. These sell-offs are usually low risk and high return, so investors rush in.'

But football clubs are often Bs

'Many football club shares are below the line. A football club is always a very risky proposition because its fortunes largely depend on how the team performs on the pitch. A company may invest in loads of players and a new ground and then lose every game. If it drops a division, the company's income from sponsorship deals, ticket sales and television rights will be vastly reduced. And most clubs don't make a profit, because player salaries and transfer fees are often bigger than the company's turnover. The combination of high risk and low return puts most football shares below the line.'

---

case study

The sad case of Millwall Holdings

It's one of my beliefs that we learn more from our mistakes than our successes. Most investors take immense pleasure bragging about their big wins. Delegates are often surprised when I openly talk about my worst-ever investment.

> Millwall Football Club was based in an area of south-east London best described as unfashionable. The most common words used to describe the area were *grim, dangerous* and *life-threatening*. Descriptions of Millwall supporters were even less flattering.
>
> So imagine the excitement when the club opened a new stadium closer to the centre of London and announced plans for a new issue of equity capital. The club was pushing for promotion to the lucrative Premier League and bought lots of good players, including two Russian internationals.
>
> I bought a line of shares at 2p each, which quickly rose to 4p. I'd doubled my money in a matter of days. I reckoned that even if Biblical plagues befell the club I would be in the money. How wrong I was to be proved.
>
> My share purchase coincided with a long string of defeats. One of the Russian players was dismissed for alcoholism, after gleefully admitting that he was on 'a honeymoon which lasted for six months'. The club dropped from promotion hopefuls to relegation certainties. No games were shown on TV and ticket prices fell. Sponsors and advertisers cut back dramatically, but the club was contractually obliged to keep paying big salaries to its players. Millwall entered administration.
>
> The shares plummeted to 0.0181p. I didn't sell them, though, because the cost of a stamp and an envelope for the share certificate was more than the worth of my total holding.

Day 1, 8.00pm – Nancy, France

Outside, floodlights suddenly shone through the sleet. Nancy station was crawling with police.

'I told you so,' said Conrad. He'd predicted that we'd be held up and was smugly happy to be proved right. It didn't seem to bother him that he'd be as late as the other passengers on the train. 'Where's your rich friend got to?'

I shrugged. And that's when I heard the scream.

The police led the passengers from the train into the empty waiting room. We sat on cold benches and waited to be interviewed. The gendarmes had commandeered the stationmaster's office as a makeshift interview room.

A man who looked like an old-fashioned bank clerk handed me a receipt for my suitcase and briefcase and a junior policeman beckoned me in to the murky room.

'What is it you do?'

'I teach people about finance.' I didn't want to spend too much time here so kept my answers as punchy as possible.

'What is your connection with Mr Abercrombie? You had lunch with Mr Abercrombie in the dining car, I believe?'

'Yes. What of it?'

'What did you talk about?'

'Risk and return.'

'Tell me what exactly.'

'Why?'

The doors swung open and the fluorescent strip lights sparked into action. A woman marched in, her heels tapping across the parquet floor. She wore a severe black business suit and was flanked by two senior policemen. She gave an order in French and my junior policeman shot up from his chair and left. My eyes adjusted to the light and I saw the newcomer more clearly.

'My name is Anisa Chabbra,' she began, as if we hadn't just spent hours together on the train. 'I work for a government agency which investigates cross-border crimes. Please tell me what you know about the missing man.'

'What missing man?' I was suddenly blank.

'Guy Abercrombie. The man who took you for lunch.'

'When did he disappear? I was waiting for him to come to my carriage.'

'What did you talk about during lunch?'

'Not much. We talked about a few old acquaintances.'

'He didn't tell you anything about his business dealings?'

'No,' I lied. 'Why would he? I hadn't seen him for a decade before bumping into him today. It was nothing more than a lucky coincidence.'

'Is this a lucky coincidence?' For the first time I noticed that the other senior policeman had been carrying my briefcase. He snapped it open on the desk. There was my laptop and there was Uli's train. And there was the analyst's report on Cal-Pan.

Anisa held up the report. 'Where did you get this?'

'I don't know. What do you want from me?'

'I want you to help us re-create Guy Abercrombie's investment portfolio. We need to trace his steps to find out what he's been doing. We need *you* to retrace his steps. I can get you out of this hole in five minutes and you can be in London for brunch tomorrow morning. But only if you promise to help me. If you don't keep your word ...'

She let the threat hang in the air.

'I don't see how I can help you.'

She was in no mood to listen to my plea of innocence. 'Guy Abercrombie made a fortune in a very short period of time. Our records show that he considered filing for personal bankruptcy eighteen months ago. And yet now he's a multimillionaire.' One of the senior policemen coughed and Anisa realised her error. 'Or at least he appeared to be.'

'What do you mean by that?'

'It seems that your friend has vanished into thin air. With a large amount of money that – strictly speaking – isn't his.'

part

two

Welcome to the jungle

4

Damn clients

1988 – Nippon Saiwai Bank, Cannon Street, London

My first job in the City came by accident. It was my second year of university and I applied for a summer job to do filing at a sleepy Japanese bank near Cannon Street station. The recruitment consultant had sent me there even though I had no previous experience, knowledge of banking or obvious administrative skills. But she told me I looked the part, and I'm still not sure whether the remark was meant as a compliment.

The marble reception hall of Nippon Saiwai was chaos. They were in the middle of a reorganisation and stacks of plastic crates made it impossible to move. A builder started drilling and a man speaking into the first mobile phone I'd ever seen told him to stop or find another job. A woman with a clipboard asked me to fill in an application form. 'You must be here to see Jerry Witts,' she said and I nodded, not knowing any better. I like to think she identified my innate ability and hidden talents but, as I sat there shaking in a twelve-quid suit from the Kidney Research charity shop and my dad's tie, I doubt it.

Jerry Witts, it turned out, was the man with the huge mobile. He didn't look up from his paperwork. 'I've no time,' he started. 'Your CV looks OK. A job for the summer, eh?'

'Yes. Er, please.'

'A quick question. Answer this and you get the job. Give me three reasons why I always choose risky investments.'

'You can make big gains. Your gains can come quickly. It's more exciting.'

'Good. Start now. Five hundred a week OK?'

There wasn't time for an answer. The previous year I had spent the summer teaching English to foreign students for £50 per week. That was a great job. Now I was getting ten times the money, but I had no idea what I was going to do. Perhaps Jerry Witts wanted someone young and strong to carry his phone.

I found out – much later – that the woman with the clipboard was meant to send me to the post room. And it was to be some time before I learned whose CV Jerry had on his desk.

The trading floor

Jerry took me under his wing that summer as I filled out spread-sheets on the bank's creaking computers. I was so green that I'd never been through a door which opened electronically. One morning Jerry slid his pass over the control. There was a beep of recognition and he beckoned me in.

'Welcome,' he said, 'to the jungle.'

It was the noise that hit me first. Then the sheer size of the open-plan floor, as big as a football pitch. Then the minions, shuttling from desk to desk carrying printouts and bacon sandwiches. Finally, the traders. Some were standing up, shouting into two phones. Others were splayed across their desks, staring at terminals and TV screens. At least two appeared to be fighting.

'I won't introduce you,' Jerry said. 'They've got no time, and they'd only be rude to you.'

'That's very kind of you to protect me, Jerry.'

Jerry laughed. 'It's not you I'm protecting. I'm facing huge reputational risk bringing a squirt like you into the lions' den.

Make sure you keep two steps behind me and don't be tempted to answer any phones.'

Conference rooms were spread around the outskirts of the trading floor. The three managing directors had offices in the corners. I stood open-mouthed as I read the signs above each row of desks – *Japanese Equities, UK Bonds, Credit Risk, Foreign Exchange, Derivatives*. Four nearly-identical men, wearing black wire spectacles and red ties, stared in silence at a graph on their Reuters screen. They smiled simultaneously when a red line crossed a green one.

'Quants,' hissed Jerry. 'Pointy-headed rocket scientists who invent whizzy trading ideas. They speak a language of their own that I don't understand.'

---

fast facts

Quants and their mysterious black boxes

What if fundamental analysis – using research and ratios to pick underpriced shares – was total bunkum? What if computers and algorithms were smarter than people?

Quant analysts believe that superior returns come from analysis of rapidly changing price information. Computers can crunch huge amounts of data in a millisecond. They are free from bias and human emotion. And they can implement thousands of trades in the time it takes you to read this sentence.

Black boxes are automatic trading systems which humans have designed but do not manage. They lead to high-frequency trading which, in turn, creates market volatility.

A ball of scrunched-up paper smacked into my right ear. A group of European equity traders took five seconds off from their careers as Masters of the Universe to laugh in unison at my pain and shock. The ball of paper was a brief research note I had written about a Spanish bank. A single Anglo-Saxon word had been written in thick black marker pen over my name.

Traders sat on long benches. Each had an individual desk covered with computers, cables, jotters and phones. The hierarchy became obvious. Senior traders were given a Bloomberg terminal each to follow news stories. A single click on a share's name revealed who was interested in buying and selling a financial instrument and at what price. I noticed that the senior traders were not the thinnest or most athletic group of men ever assembled. By 10 in the morning their desks were covered with wrappers from McDonald's, KFC and Arcoboleno, an Italian deli that was to become my favourite.

Spreadsheet monkeys

More junior traders clustered around a shared Bloomberg. Deals were fed into a separate monitor running a Reuters trading platform. Their poor clerks had to live with a single computer each. One of the clerks had the slogan *spreadsheet monkey* emblazoned on the back of his chair.

A senior trader was berating a junior who looked so young he might have been on a day release scheme from a local secondary school.

'There are a million things you need to know about these IBM shares before you buy them. Can you list me ten fundamentals?'

The junior started off cockily. 'Share price, earnings per share, dividend per share, P/E ratio, dividend yield.'

❝ What secret do you know that the market doesn't? ❞

The senior interrupted him. 'Rubbish. Everyone in the market knows all of those factors. What secret do you know that the market doesn't?'

The junior scratched his head. He pondered for five seconds, which seemed an eternity in the infernal hubbub of the trading floor. At last he spoke. 'Nothing' was all that he said.

'Then don't do the trade. Got it?'

'Yes.'

'Good work. Now get me a sausage bagel, fresh tomato, pepper but no salt. You can forget about trading until you get my breakfast order 100 per cent right for a week.'

Proprietary trading

Jerry's stamina was unnerving. He was always first in the office, and had a stock of pithy phrases to show that he was the king of the early-risers.

'Hi,' he'd say to anyone coming in at 6.30. 'Great to see someone else wants to be a winner. But remember, it's the early bird that gets me the coffee.' If you turned up at 6.45 you'd get these questions: 'Tube not working? Or have you come straight from a nightclub?'

Pity the fools who tried to get round Jerry's sarcasm by offering him a coffee at 7.15. 'Coffee. No thanks. I've been drinking it all morning.' At 7.30 it was, 'Time for lunch?' At 8am it would be a curt 'Good evening.'

But in those days I never saw him blow up or lose his self-composure. His verbal attacks were his way of releasing stress, and I preferred them to those of other MDs, who regularly bounced their phones on to my wall. And I found him genuinely funny; especially, of course, when he was cutting down someone other than me. He would help me by delivering short sermons in the lift.

'Proprietary trading uses the bank's own capital. Traders buy and sell financial assets to create a profit which belongs to the bank. Traders always believe they are smarter than other investors (especially their clients) because of their superior intellectual power and the huge breadth of their market knowledge. That's normally rubbish, but there are some areas where Saiwai has a huge advantage over the market. Our derivative deals, for example, are so complex that you need a PhD in maths to understand them.'

Another time Jerry explained how investment banks made their money.

'Different investment banks may look very similar to outsiders. They normally split into three main areas of business: *investment banking and advisory, asset management* and *trading*. Within these broad groupings, however, there are many different functions. Some banks may have a huge trading floor, others may be more focused on asset management.

'Investment banks carry out financial advisory work for clients. This section of the investment bank – sometimes known as *mergers and acquisitions* or the *investment banking division* – is responsible for raising capital via share and bond issues. These transactions are extremely lucrative and banks will fight to the death for a client mandate.'

It's raining middlemen

'Investment banking is a classic middleman business. You can think of it as a simple diagram. On the left-hand side we have institutional investors. Insurers, pension fund managers and the treasuries of big businesses create huge volumes of work for investment banks. They are cash-rich and need to invest. Institutional investors are assumed to know their way around finance, so in most countries they will get less protection from regulators even though the amount of money at risk is massive.

'Think of the pressure facing a pension fund. It receives your pension payment, plus the payments of all the people in your department, and all the other people in your firm, plus money from people who work at suppliers and customers and competitors, and their neighbours, wives, husbands and mates from the gym. Every month the pension fund has a mountain of money to invest.'

Jerry encouraged me to understand what kept Saiwai's clients awake at night. He used this diagram to show how investment banks make money.

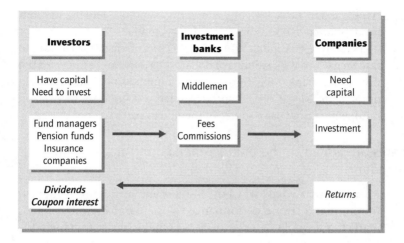

'Putting it in a bank account and playing golf for the next forty years isn't an option. Decisions on risk tolerance and asset allocation have to be made. The pension fund will have a list of investment banks which can advise it on equities, bonds, derivatives and alternative investments.'

The lift stopped. Outside was the junior trader who I last saw being torn apart by his boss for screwing up the breakfast order. It was clear from the pile of pizza boxes balanced between his burning hands that progress had not been rapid.

'Who's that?' I asked.

Jerry pushed the shut button so the lift wouldn't open. 'He's called Jonathan Spurrier. He's as much use as a chocolate fireguard.' Without missing a beat Jerry continued with his explanation.

'Analysts are paid to generate ideas which salespeople can present to clients. The investment bank makes money by charging commissions to its clients. A dream call for a salesman is a switch, where the pension fund sells Portuguese bonds and buys Danish derivatives with the same money. This generates both a selling and a buying commission for the bank – and, of course, the salesman and the analyst.

'Think about the right-hand side of my diagram. Here the pension fund is offered bonds in the primary market. These businesses desperately need capital. When the directors of MegaCorp A want to buy MegaCorp B for trillions of dollars they don't have, they call the investment bank. MegaCorp A issues a jumbo bond with the help of the bank. MegaCorp A contracts to pay a coupon to the pension fund, which now has a source of income to pay to its pensioners.'

Shares are issued to the primary market and trade in the secondary

I learned that when you buy a share you're hoping to benefit from either a strong performance by the company or the stock market as a whole. If a company becomes a leader in its sector – as, for example, Apple is now – it will make greater and greater earnings so people will pay more to buy a share. Greater earnings will eventually lead to bigger dividends as well.

Jerry also taught me to distinguish between the primary and the secondary market.

'A private company does not have shares listed on a stock exchange. Private companies are normally owned by relatively few people and tend to expand organically, re-investing profits to buy another shop or a new piece of machinery. But directors might want growth to be more rapid or they might want to cash in some of their own shares. This is the *primary market*, where an investment bank turns the private company into a public company. You may have heard this referred to as *going public*, *listing on the stock exchange* and *initial public offering* (which is always abbreviated to IPO).

'The *secondary market* is where shares are bought and sold and traded. Unkind critics call the secondary market a *marketplace for second-hand securities*. Every time a share changes hands, there are commissions to be made.'

Day 2, 12.33pm – St Pancras Station, London

The train was met by screams and the flash of cameras. Anisa saw a scrum of photographers and, just for a second, wondered if the press had been alerted about the disappearance. But, with a sigh of relief, she realised that film stars, as well as ordinary mortals, had been caught up in the no-flight ban. There was Tom Cruise and there was Cameron Diaz and two steps behind them stood Kevin Bacon.

Rumour had it that Bacon had lost an eight-figure sum after investing in Bernie Madoff's notorious funds. Madoff had promised absolute safety with a high level of income. Why hadn't Madoff's clients – property magnates, powerful politicians, super-wealthy retirees – realised that such a combination was impossible? And how many more frauds are left to be uncovered?

---

case study

The Madoff scandal

The most famous inmate at Butner medium-security prison is prisoner 61727–054, more commonly known as Bernie Madoff. In December 2008 he confessed to his family that his massively successful investment fund and brokerage had been a fraud. He was sentenced to 150 years in Butner for swindling $65 billion.

Madoff worked hard to appear respectable. As well as sitting on the boards of many charities he was at one time a chairman of the Nasdaq stock market and vice-president of the National Association of Securities Dealers. Madoff's reputation, credibility and fantastic contacts meant very few sceptics. He kept his clientele exclusive and many of his investors regarded an account with Madoff as a badge of social acceptance. In retrospect, their trust appears ludicrous.

The public side of Madoff's business was on the 18th and 19th floors of Manhattan's Lipstick Building, where ringing phones and shouting traders gave the impression of a healthy operation. But a quick trip down the stairs to floor 17 would have revealed the

> shambolic, paper-strewn centre of the fraud where Madoff employed a coterie of selected friends and close relatives. Regulators first investigated Madoff's funds as early as 2002 but failed to crack down on him. Indeed, Madoff was surprised his crimes were not discovered earlier. A whistleblower at the US Securities and Exchange Commission described the regulator as being 'staffed by 3,500 chickens' who were no match for a sly fox like Madoff.
>
> Madoff ran his fund as a simple Ponzi scheme. As new clients paid in funds, Madoff paid their money out to existing investors. For all his talk of clever strategies and sophisticated trading algorithms, very few real trades were actually conducted. Frauds don't have to be hi-tech or complex to be successful. There's more information on Ponzi schemes in Chapter 18.
>
> **Weird fact** – Madoff has a couple of new prison nicknames. His fellow con-artists call him either 'The Godfather' or 'The Don' in recognition of his criminal skills.

Anisa had come to St Pancras to make sure I hadn't run.

The French police had accompanied me across the Channel. For a horrible couple of hours I had thought they were going to put me in the cells overnight. Instead they had dropped me off at a small guest house in Nancy and picked me up in the morning. I didn't speak enough French to ask them whether I was a witness or a suspect but they hadn't felt the need to handcuff me.

We walked in silence to her car. How had I gone from being a happy and contented training consultant to an accessory in a murder case?

Anisa began. 'I hope you appreciate how hard it was to get you back. The French police are convinced you're implicated.'

'What do you want from me, Anisa? If you really thought I was involved you'd have left me there.'

She bit her lower lip and looked in the rear view mirror. 'OK.

Here's the deal. I've told my boss that I can figure out Guy Abercrombie's crimes. He thinks I'm a hotshot economics expert but my skills are, shall we say, a little rusty.'

'So?'

'You help with a crash course in finance. I do my best to save your skin.'

'No. Guy Abercrombie has nothing to do with me. He was an ex-student of mine and I hadn't seen him for ten years. I don't know how he made his money or who his enemies are. I have to go to New York to deliver a course in two days. I want to go home and see my nephew and go to sleep and wake up and forget all this has happened. And I want you and whatever department you work for to leave me alone.'

'Of course,' she said smiling. 'A quick question first.'

'Yes.'

'Would you like me to call the police and get you on the next train back to France?'

'No.'

'I doubt whether a great big *deported* stamp is what you want in your passport. I don't think that will go down so well with your international clients.'

5

An equitable solution

Who predicted futurology?

I finished my final year at uni and returned to Jerry the day after. Saiwai was doing well, and my salary was three times what my classmates were getting. The job was fun and Jerry continued to share his hard-won knowledge with me.

'An investor', Jerry told me, 'buys shares for two types of return. There's the capital gain and there's the dividend payments. Now imagine the situation: you've got a profitable company which can either pay you a dividend or can keep the money. Investors who prefer the cash now are called value investors. They want a steady flow of dividends.

'The other group of investors have a different perspective. We call them growth investors. A growth stock is an investment which offers superior return potential compared to other shares in the market.

'Often growth companies have an innovative new product or something unique that the company offers. But growth can also come from other areas.

'If people get married later than in previous generations, the demand for small flats and single-serving ready-made meals will grow. This is an example of demographic change.

'Sometimes growth comes because of regulation. If you're in a country where smoking is banned overnight, then the sale of smoking patches or nicotine gum will automatically increase. It's the gifted analyst who sees that the law change will also lead to a growth in peanuts being sold because people who are drinking and can't smoke need something to do with their hands.

> **❝ If you want to make money from growth stocks, it's always important to see the big trend ❞**

'Occasionally you get a completely new market, something you've never really thought of before. Recent health scares have led people to go for higher quality cuts of meat, so suddenly there's a demand for organically reared meat. If you want to make money from growth stocks, it's always important to see the big trend.

'That's why we employ futurologists, who are people who are employed to predict changes. A futurologist thinks like this. The government announces a cut in the budget for school meals. Children will therefore eat poorer quality meals and develop a taste for cheaper food laden with salt, sugar and chemical preservatives. Twenty years down the line many of these children will develop type 2 diabetes. The gifted futurologist looks for sectors that will benefit from this change: pharmaceuticals, healthcare, hospital construction, insulin production.'

I learned more about Jonathan Spurrier from the Saiwai rumour mill. Some said he was the son of one of Saiwai's top clients. Others hinted that he was related to the royal family. Despite an expensive education at several second-division public schools, together with two stints at A-level crammer colleges, Spurrier seemed to have failed every exam since his cycling proficiency. In a rare moment of self-analysis, he told me that he didn't want to go to university anyway, since he was now older than many of the lecturers.

He had wonderful clothes and impeccable brogues. But he probably had help putting them on.

One thing was certain. Jerry Witts hated everything about Jonathan. Later – much later – I was to discover why.

Stock-pickers of the world unite and take over

Jerry sat down with me for twenty minutes at the end of each day.

'Value companies are mature businesses which produce a steady stream of earnings. Their *profit after tax* every year is normally very consistent. The most important number for the analyst is the *earnings per share*, referred to as the *EPS* by those in the know. The first thing an analyst does is take the profit after tax and divide it by the number of shares.'

Jerry dug into his blazer and flourished the thickest Montblanc I'd ever seen. 'Let's say the company makes profit after tax of £10,000 and there are 4,000 shares in issue. Each share makes £2.50.'

Earnings per share		
A	Profit after tax	£10,000
B	Number of shares	4,000
C = A/B	Earnings per share	£2.50

'For each share you own, the company has made you £2.50. However, it's extremely unlikely that the company will pay 100 per cent of this money out in dividends. Some money will be paid out in dividends, but a proportion will be retained within the company. Finding out what proportion of profits leaves the company in the form of dividend is vital for investors.

'Our company pays £1.50 in dividend for every share that you have. We call that the *DPS*, short for *dividend per share*. If you divide the DPS by the EPS you have the *payout ratio*, which tells you how much of the earnings (the profit after tax) is paid out in dividends.'

The payout ratio calculates how much profit is paid out as dividends

Payout ratio		
D	Dividend per share	£1.50
C	Earnings per share	£2.50
E = D/C	Payout ratio	60%

'Fast-growth companies don't pay out dividends because they need all their money. Our strategy is simple. We search for companies with a very high payout ratio. We market the fund at older investors, who are far more interested in steady income than capital gain. My analysts make a list of all available companies and place them in order of payout ratio. I use my own experience as a stock-picker to select thirty or forty companies which I believe will continue with a high payout ratio. My plan is to hold the shares for a long time.'

The hapless Jonathan Spurrier was increasingly the target of Jerry's barbs. Jonathan was once on the phone, trying hard to raise some more funds from a tough-talking individual. Jonathan was useless at picking investments and hated explaining just how badly his choices had performed.

'I want you to know,' said Jonathan to his potential client, 'this is the best way to a small fortune.'

Jerry, walking through the graduate area, shouted out, 'The best way to a small fortune is to give a large fortune to Jonathan Spurrier.'

We all died laughing, except for Jonathan and, presumably, his furious client.

Another time Jonathan had just finished a call to a pension fund. The client, Jonathan informed us, was looking at the problem of early retirement amongst the very successful and relatively young.

'According to their success demographics, I'm an excellent candidate for early retirement,' Jonathan proudly announced.

'When were you thinking?' I asked.

Before Jonathan could answer Jerry said, 'If you want, I'll arrange it for this afternoon.'

The dividend yield measures the income from a share

Jerry explained to me how he kept the Saiwai client base happy.

'My analysts focus on the *dividend yield*. The dividend yield shows the relationship between the dividend per share and the share price. Our shares paid a dividend of £1.50 and the share price was £60. What this means is that every year, if these numbers were to stay the same, we'd make 2.5 per cent just on the dividend. Remember, you're only looking here at the income on the share, not at any changes in the share price.'

Dividend yield

D	Dividend per share	£1.50
F	Price per share	£60
G = D/F	Dividend yield	2.5%

Jerry explained how they picked their companies. 'Any firm offering a high dividend yield is perfect for our clients. Anything that has a very low dividend yield – a start-up company or a company that is growing rapidly – we avoid like the plague.'

Jerry's strategy had been extremely successful for many years. I asked him what other companies he avoided and he told me the fund never considered a small company.

'What is your definition of small?'

'A company where the *market capitalisation* is less than £200 million. The market cap is the value of the company on the stock exchange. It's the number of shares multiplied by the share price.'

Market capitalisation		
B	Number of shares	4,000
F	Price per share	£60
H = B × F	Market cap	£240,000

'My next investment criterion was to find companies that appeared to be unloved or forgotten by the stock market. I deliberately launched my fund as a clear alternative to the highly volatile technology funds that were popular at the time. I concentrate on highly profitable organisations which provide a stable rate of return. My boring carthorses are the diametric opposite of start-ups, which are volatile and normally loss-making.'

The P/E ratio tells us what investors think about different companies

'My final fund selection technique is to analyse the relationship between a company's share price and its EPS. This is captured in the *P/E ratio*, which is the ratio of share price to EPS. For example, our company has a share price of £60 and the earnings per share are £2.50. This means that investors in the market are willing to pay twenty-four times the earnings to buy the share.'

P/E ratio		
F	Price per share	£60
C	Earnings per share	£2.50
I = F/C	P/E ratio	24x

'A high P/E ratio usually means that investors believe a company's earnings are going to rocket. The higher the P/E, the higher the premium investors are prepared to pay for the stock. Do you remember those factors we talked about: new product, demographic change, regulation? If a company benefits from these, its P/E will rise.'

'Normally a low P/E ratio suggests a value company. Solid and dependable, but the share price is never going to zoom.'

Value, growth, neither, both

Jerry showed me a table with two companies.

Lucky Star Bet is a gambling company which had recently launched a very popular collection of spread bets on football. Gamblers could put their money on the exact time a goalkeeper first took off his gloves or the number of times the ball hit goalposts. The company spent a fortune in advertising and had made a heavy investment in computer systems and software. Lucky Star Bet had just reported its first earnings of 10p per share.

Great Northern Power supplies gas, electricity and water to consumers in the north-east of England. The company had been running since 1953. Its EPS was also 10p per share.

The strange thing was that Lucky Star's share price was 400p and Great Northern's was only 100p. Why were shares that made the same earnings priced so differently?

	Lucky Star Bet	Great Northern Power
Share price	400p	100p
EPS	10p	10p
P/E ratio	40x	10x

Why were investors willing to pay well over the odds to buy companies like Lucky Star? The hope was that next year's EPS would be 15p, and then 25p and then maybe 50p as it became a dominant player in the market. If this happened the share price would zoom and the investors will be rewarded with big capital gains.

'That's absolutely crucial,' Jerry continued. 'A high P/E ratio is something which the market ascribes to a high-growth company.

The greater the expectations of growth in earnings, the higher the P/E.

'With good old Great Northern Power, investors expect the earnings next year to be 10p, maybe 9.5p or maybe 10.5p. It's the sort of company that isn't going to have a massive change in earnings either way. It's steady.'

---

case study

The Google growth story

Google funded its expansion via an issue of shares priced at $85. The company's EPS at the time was $1.14, so the P/E ratio on listing day was 74.6x (which is $85 divided by $1.14). Over the next six months, the shares soared to $185, which meant that the P/E was a massive 162.3x ($185 divided by the same EPS of $1.14).

(Please note that it's common practice to calculate the P/E to one decimal place and to follow it with the 'x', which is analyst shorthand for 'multiple'.)

Why were investors prepared to buy shares at such a massive premium? Because they believed that Google could massively grow earnings.

Google is the world's most visited website. Stop for a second and just consider how important that makes the company. The acquisition of DoubleClick meant that Google was the first company to make proper profits from online adverts, which have now superseded traditional media adverts. Continual spending on research and development keeps driving people to the company's websites. Buying YouTube, the world's third most popular website, was another revenue-enhancing masterstroke.

Have you ever heard anyone say 'I Binged him' or 'I Yahooed her?' No, of course you haven't. Google belongs to that select group of companies − Hoover, Xerox − whose name has become a verb.

Day 2, 2.30pm – My office, Covent Garden, London

'Where on earth have you been?' Anisa screamed down the phone. 'I've been calling you for hours.'

'I'm writing up some notes. What's the emergency?'

'I've got a meeting with a City contact. It's someone I knew from uni. He says he works in the front office. Is that the side closest to the road?'

'No Anisa, not always. Let me send you something to read.'

I heard the slam of a car door. 'Good,' Anisa said as she flipped her phone shut, leaving me with my head in my hands. The last thing I needed, as I struggled to concentrate on course preparation, was Anisa Chabbra bothering me.

---

fast facts

Office politics – the front, back and middle offices at a bank

The internal workings of an investment bank are split into three areas or 'offices'.

The *front office* deals directly with clients. Staff work as corporate financiers, sales people, investment managers, traders and research analysts. The *back office* is responsible for checking transactions. An essential part of this process is settlement and clearing. Back office staff must ensure that each and every trade results in a movement of cash and/or securities in or out of the bank. Also included in the back office are technology, HR and accounting.

If you're into football analogies, the front office is where the glory-hunting goal-hangers strut their stuff. The back office is for goalkeepers and hard-tackling defenders. However, you don't always get a strong sense that the front and back office are on the same team. The front office looks down at the back office as full of annoying fact-checkers who get in the way of their fun. The back office views the front office with derision. They are over-paid and under-talented prima donnas who can barely tie their own bootlaces without bankrupting the firm. The truth depends on where you work.

The *middle office* is where you'll find the bank's treasury, finance and risk management divisions. The middle office is slightly undervalued by both the front and back offices but it's growing in importance. Here, for example, you'll find the team which estimates the bank's entire credit risk, a subject we return to in Chapter 22.

6

Promises, promises

Looking back, I can now see that Jerry's influence was not always positive.

He started earlier and stayed later than anyone in the office. But his lunchtimes – and waistline – were expanding to compensate. I learned not to expect much wisdom from him when he stumbled back from The Blackfriars pub at three in the afternoon. Mind you, he did teach me about trading derivatives, even if his method was a little peculiar.

I could smell the gin even before I entered his glass office. Jerry stretched back in his chair and yawned. 'I have two questions for you,' he said, scratching a match along the underside of his mahogany table.

'What are they?'

The naked position

'Do you want to learn about derivatives? And do you want to see Brenda Leckie take her clothes off?'

Brenda was our lovely, but rather frumpy, head of compliance. She sat on the other side of the glass partition, seemingly oblivious to Jerry and his silly plots. 'Yes to the derivatives but no to the clothes.'

'Tough.' Jerry lit his cigarette on the third attempt, his hand fluttering unsteadily in front of his face. 'You can't have one without the other.'

'OK.' Well, it was Friday afternoon and no work was being done. And Jerry, of course, was my boss and mentor, so it was smart to keep on his right side.

'Good man.' Jerry rummaged in a desk drawer and pulled out the remote control for the air conditioning which had been installed as part of Saiwai's refurbishment. He angled it towards Brenda's gold-fish bowl office. 'How long do you reckon?'

'I doubt you can do it in less than sixty seconds, Jerry. Any time after that, you owe me.' If Jerry could make Brenda remove her jacket in less than sixty seconds he'd win. If it took longer, victory would be mine. But it wasn't simply a matter of bragging rights. For each second below sixty, I needed to pay Jerry. And he'd have to pay me for each second above the magic number.

All that remained was to figure out what each second was worth. 'How much per second?' he asked.

'A pound?'

'Make it ten.' In a way he'd won the bet already. Ten pounds a second meant nothing to a man of Jerry's wealth. For me, it meant the difference between living the high life for a month or staying in every night with cornflakes and TV.

He winked when he saw my worried face. 'Start the clock!' he shouted.

Fifteen seconds ticked past, and there was no reaction from the bowl. Jerry saw me smile, and immediately raised the stakes. 'Fancy your chances, do you? Want to make it more interesting? Twenty pounds a second?'

This was real money at stake now. Enough to hurt. Like a fool I nodded agreement. Twenty-five seconds gone. No movement from the comfortably settled Brenda Leckie, but then her PA, a lad from Manchester called Dan or Stan or something, blew out a puff of air.

'Look at him waving his hands around!' shrieked Jerry. 'Must be getting mighty hot in there.'

Thirty-five, thirty-six, thirty-seven. Please Brenda, I was silently begging, keep your jacket on. Jerry bared his teeth, keeping his gaze fixed on head of compliance. 'Come on,' he muttered, 'it must be eighty degrees in there.'

Forty seconds. I'd been holding my breath because of the tension. My maximum exposure was £400, which was £20 multiplied by twenty seconds. And after that, my upside was unlimited.

Forty-nine seconds in and disaster struck. No! Brenda picked up a manila file and fanned herself. 'Looks like you'll be making a visit to the cash point soon.'

'Don't be so sure, Jerry. In six – no, five – seconds I'll be in the kill zone.'

'Don't think so, mate.' And, immediately he'd finished, Brenda suddenly stood up and struggled to slip her green jacket from her bulky shoulders.

'Stop the clock!' Jerry shouted out. 'I make that four seconds. You owe me eighty quid. Cash only, I'm afraid.'

But I'd stopped listening. A woman with long black hair elegantly waved her manicured hands in front of her beautiful face. The first time I saw Perrine's face was while I was losing money.

Sad to say, this was to prove an omen.

The time value of money

Perrine had been brought up in Paris, Madrid and Milan. She'd studied art history in Turin and philosophy at Columbia. From a purely rational point of view, it wasn't entirely clear what Perrine brought to Saiwai in terms of hard business skills. But I – like 90 per cent of Saiwai's male staff – had fallen head over heels in love.

I smiled every time she mangled English, which was her third or fourth language. Jerry was playing *devil's avocado* with the market. Old-time risk-averse investors were *dinosaurs voting for Christmas*.

Jerry – who never missed a trick – teased me mercilessly. But his cruellest trick was to assign me to be Perrine's mentor. I blushed at the very thought of her and stammered in her presence. I bought a book called *The Time Value of Money Made Easy* and prepared our first lesson.

'This topic is much easier than you think.' I imagined that would be a good opening: it showed I was confident and it was designed to relax Perrine.

'No it isn't,' she said. You know you've got it bad when you find a girl's sulking attractive.

'All you need to do is imagine you lend €10 to a friend for a year.' I thought Euros would make me seem more Continental in her eyes. The currency hadn't even been invented at this stage so I thought I'd also look pretty cutting-edge. 'Why does your friend need to pay back more than he borrowed?'

'What's my friend called?'

'Eh?' The question threw me. 'Anything you like.'

'Good. I will call him Armin.'

It sounds stupid but I was jealous of this imaginary Armin. In fact, it sounds really pathetic, doesn't it?

The promise of money is not worth the same as money today

I went on. 'There are three reasons why Armin will need to pay you back more.'

1. Inflation

This erodes the value of money. Suppose inflation is very low at 2 per cent. If Armin gives you €10 after a year, you'll really only receive €9.80. What's happened to the 20c? Inflation has bitten off a chunk.

Inflation erodes the value of savings and hyper-inflation can destroy a country's economy. In 2008 inflation reached

231,150,888 per cent per year in Zimbabwe. (That was the official estimate, which probably understated the real figure.)

2. Opportunity cost

Armin has borrowed your €10 for a year, and that stopped you from doing anything with the money. You need a reward for renting your money out to Armin. How about the interest you would have made if you'd tied up the money in a bank deposit for twelve months? Perhaps 3 per cent would be enough?

3. Risk of the borrower

This is a very variable factor. A lender will charge more if they think the borrower is risky.

What are the signs of a bad bet?

- Not long in a new job? (Perrine ticked that one).
- Already got big debts (tick).
- Credit cards that can't be paid off within a month (tick).

But Armin has none of these problems. His individual risk as a borrower was only 5 per cent. This number reflects the riskiness of the borrower. It varies from one borrower to another, and will be much higher if the lender has doubts about being paid back.

After my explanation, Perrine added these three elements together.

She begins with inflation …	2%
… then adds opportunity cost …	3%
… and the risk of the borrower.	5%
The total is the cost of borrowing	10%

Armin was going to pay interest at the rate of 10 per cent per annum.

It's just the same as compounding. If you lend €10 and think Armin is a 10 per cent risk, he will need to pay back €11 next year. That's the initial €10 multiplied by 1.1, because Armin's going to have to pay you 10 per cent interest for borrowing your money.

	Compounding	
A	Money borrowed	€10
B	Interest rate	10%
C = A × (1+B)	Amount to pay back	€11.00

'Perrine, let me ask you a question. You can have €10 now, cash in your hands. Or you can have the promise of €10 in exactly one year's time. Which option do you prefer?'

> **your borrower may go bust, go on the run, spend all their cash on drink or just plain die**

She considered for a second. 'Everyone should choose the cash now. It's certain, you've got it, there's no chance of the borrower not paying. The promise is just that. It's not guaranteed, and your borrower may go bust, go on the run, spend all their cash on drink or just plain die. The lender needs compensation because of these added risks. And the longer you lend the money, the more compensation you will demand because there is more time for bad things to happen.'

'So what does this mean for bankers?'

Perrine delicately chewed the top of her pen.

'€10 today does *not* have the same value as the promise of €10 in one year. Since all of us prefer to take €10 today, it must follow that €10 next year is worth less than €10 today.'

'How much less?'

'I don't know.'

'Well, let me tell you.' She smiled at me. Perrine actually smiled at me! This teaching lark was better than I had ever imagined.

Discounting is compounding in reverse

Perrine was determined to get the next bit done and dusted. She knew that the total risk of lending money was worth a return of 10 per cent. She also knew she would be paid €10 in one year's time. But what was that future payment worth to her today?

She divided the payment of €10 by 1.1 to discount the value of the repayment in the future. Why 1.1? Because it's 1 plus 10 per cent.

The 10 per cent is called the discount rate. And 1 divided by 1.1, which is 90.9 per cent, is the discount factor. It's like saying the promise of €10 in one year is only worth 90.9 per cent. It follows that €10 in one year is only worth €9.09 today.

	Discounting	
A	Cash flow at the end of Year 1	€10
B	Discount rate	10%
$C = 1/(1 + B)$	Discount factor	90.9%
$D = A \times C$	Value of cash flow to us now	€9.09

She sketched out a couple of simple diagrams. In the first, Armin borrows €10 and has to pay back €11. The difference (€1) is the interest. As you move from today (on the left) to the future (the right) the value of the amount to repay increases.

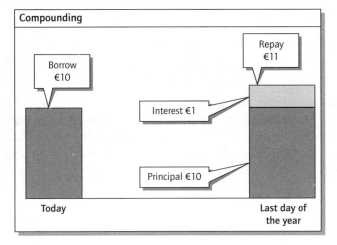

Compounding

Borrow €10

Repay €11

Interest €1

Principal €10

Today

Last day of the year

Another chew of the pen and then she had a revelation.

'Discounting is just the opposite of compounding!'

You move from a time in the future (on the right) to today (on the left). The promise of €10 in a year is only worth €9.09 today.

'I get it!' she screamed. 'At last, I get it!'

Our eyes met. Was she going to leap across the desk and hug me? Was she going to give me a great big smacker or a refined peck on the cheek? Was she … well, no she wasn't.

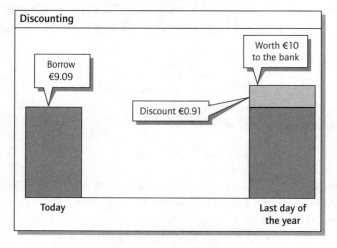

Around this time I noticed a new cynicism about Jerry. There was a hardening where once there was humour. He told me once over the top of his drink: 'If you can smile when things go wrong, it's probably because there's someone you can blame.' But there was no cackling laugh, just a gallows grin.

The bank's younger staff started to go to the movies en masse at the end of the week. We started with *The Bonfire of the Vanities*. This fantastically moving novel of greed and personal morality was turned into the worst-ever film about Wall Street you will ever sleep through.

The Bonfire of the Vanities

Tom Wolfe's Dickensian tale centres on Sherman McCoy. He's one of the Masters of the Universe, a select band who control the financial markets. Upset at his measly $999,997 salary, McCoy finds solace in the arms of his gold-digging mistress. Wolfe brilliantly captures the decisive nature of wealth as the different worlds of New York collide.

There's a moral dimension to *The Bonfire of the Vanities* which many of today's financial thrillers lack. Wall Street, Tokyo and the City are not run by cocaine-snorting, wise-cracking hipsters. People working in banks are under enormous pressure to perform. Fear and greed may blind them to the consequences of their decisions. Sherman McCoy realises that his privileged WASP world is many more times dishonest than the rough streets of New York where he pays for his crimes. He experiences a moment of clarity at the end of the book when he understands that even a Master of the Universe is not exempt from judgement. Everybody, no matter how rich or how poor, must take responsibility for their actions.

This absolute clunker of a movie is now mostly remembered for Melanie Griffith's real-life breast augmentation surgery midway through shooting. Tom Hanks plays the aggressive WASP bond trader McCoy as a lovable family man with a low-level mid-life crisis. Bruce Willis is hideously miscast as an alcoholic investigative journalist with a transatlantic accent which suggests an upbringing in London, New York, Los Angeles and, quite possibly, Cardiff.

Film fact – Wolfe (who didn't pen the screenplay) was paid $750,000 for the film rights. Which is more than some of the book's Masters of the Universe were pulling in.

Wall Street Blues

Perrine and I went to see an Oliver Stone double bill, with Jonathan Spurrier tagging along like a great big gooseberry. *Wall Street* was as far removed from our jobs as was humanely possible.

There was no jumping out of helicopters and into jacuzzis for me. Mostly it was copying spreadsheets and trying to plug a memory card into my computers. Sometimes I envied the post room boys I so nearly joined.

But *Wall Street* was really good on the details of insider trading. Bud Fox, played by the sane and reasonable Charlie Sheen, is tempted by money supremo Gordon Gekko to come up with insider information. He sacrifices the company where his father works in a deal with the devilish financier. The avaricious yet naive Fox loses his soul in his quest for big bucks. But the rewards are certainly enticing. From my seat in the Odeon Panton Street I was entranced by the speed of Bud's transformation. One minute he's cold-calling stroppy clients with a weak sales pitch, the next he's suggestively making sushi with his trophy girlfriend in a massive penthouse overlooking Manhattan.

The second film was *Platoon*, which became something of an in joke for Perrine and me. The poster screamed *The First Casualty of War is Truth!* But, as we were slowly beginning to realise, truth was actually under serious attack from Jerry's drug use.

You're probably now expecting a big section about wild City boys out of their skulls on cocaine. I'm sorry to disappoint you. I saw very little use of recreational drugs while I worked in finance, especially not on school nights. And Jerry most certainly wasn't snorting gak from his desktop. No, his choice of poison was much more prosaic but ultimately just as dangerous.

Jerry was hooked on prescription drugs, washed down with vodka. He claimed to have hurt his back playing rugby years ago and often groaned when he stood up. It sounds stupid but no one had any idea about how dangerous a diet of aspirin, paracetamol and codeine could be. His desk drawer rattled every time he pulled it open. I began to notice airline miniatures of Smirnoff, wrapped up in research reports and tossed into the wastepaper basket. Like all true alkies, he was never seen with a glass in his hand. Once, late at night, I found a couple of bottles of the super-strength sleeping pill, temazepam, in his office.

But how I got into his office is a story for later. As are some more details on insider trading.

Day 2, 4.15pm – My offices, Covent Garden, London

I have one longstanding client, a firm of Magic Circle lawyers, which I use as a barometer of where investor sentiment is heading. During the boom times their litigators want to know about mergers and acquisitions, private equity and hedge funds. In the years after a crash they focus on bad debt and company collapses. And now, suddenly, they needed to know everything about bonds.

The head of training, a harassed woman called Donna, called. Could I do a session on fixed income ASAP? My mind, obviously, was occupied with other concerns and I had to rehearse for the big presentation in New York. But, given the problems I was facing, it might well be advantageous to have a roomful of lawyers in my contacts list.

'When do you want me to speak?' I asked her.

'Can you be here in twenty minutes?'

'Of course.'

Day 2, 4.45pm – Broadgate, London

When I got to their offices Donna met me by the lift. She told me why the demand was so urgent.

'The senior partner's been called by a fund which buys new issues of corporate bonds. Apparently the fund is unhappy with the market knowledge of their present lawyers. They want to see us ASAP. But we aren't exactly experts in this field, either.'

'When are your guys meeting the fund?' I looked down on to Liverpool Street Station.

'As soon as you've finished training them!'

My phone started to ring. Anisa's name came up. I decided not to answer it. That was a mistake.

'Donna, give me a minute.'

I could see the hungry lawyers waiting for me. The temptation in this situation is to condense everything you know and speak really really quickly. But no one ever learns from a trainer who's flipping through slides saying, 'Oh, you can read that later' or 'We haven't got time to do this.' It's far better to strip everything down to a single page of essentials.

I made a list of bullet points, straightened my tie and strolled in.

'Listen,' I began. 'I'm going to tell you the minimum you need to know about bonds to get through your first client meeting. And not a single word more.'

Income and safety

'Steady income and capital preservation are the two factors which distinguish bonds from any other forms of investments. Most pension funds are big bond investors. They want lump sums to make payments to pensioners when they retire and then they want steady income to provide the regular monthly payments for the pensioners. And they want safety as well.

> **Steady income and capital preservation are the two factors which distinguish bonds**

'Let's look at the bond from the point of view of the issuing company. A bond is a contract which guarantees certain cash flows to the investor.' At the mention of the word 'contract' the lawyers, happy to be on familiar ground, relaxed their tense shoulders. 'The issuing company has to pay the agreed contractual amount, no matter how well or how badly the business is doing. It doesn't matter if sales are going through the roof, or the company's products have fallen out of favour, they have to pay the coupon.'

Bonds issues need an underwriter and a syndicate

'Corporate bonds are issued with the help of an *underwriter*, normally an investment bank. The underwriter advises the company on how much money it can raise in the market and the interest it will have to pay on its borrowings. A gifted underwriter will also know how investors want the bond to be structured. For instance, some investors will be focused on short maturity bonds so they do not have a lengthy exposure to the risks of the company. Other investors – the pension fund comes to mind – might have a thirty- or even a forty-year time frame.

'The underwriter also takes responsibility for organising a *syndicate*. This is a group of middlemen which take the bonds from the issuing company and get them to the ultimate investors. Successful syndicates have strong market contacts and, of course, a commission-hungry sales force. Any syndicate member that can't get its bonds to investors assumes market risk, and the possible losses which that entails.'

I looked at my watch. There were two, maybe three minutes to go. It was a bad time for the first question of the session.

'Why would the shareholders of a company prefer to raise capital via bonds rather than shares? Surely, once the cash is in their bank account it doesn't matter.'

Bonds allow a company to keep control

'One huge advantage for shareholders is that they can issue many bonds without giving away any control of the company. And issuing bonds is much, much quicker than issuing equity. For example, if a company has done an issue in the past, it may only take them forty-eight hours to get more money. What domestic investors don't realise is that the bond market is absolutely massive and there's a huge investor base around the world.

'Having fixed interest and principal repayment dates in the calendar helps companies plan their cash flow. It doesn't guarantee the company will have the money but it does focus people on running their business profitably. The bond market is very low profile in comparison to the equity market and rarely hits the headlines. It's a market for seasoned professionals not for beginners, so the regulators apply the lightest of light touches.'

The head partner nodded in agreement. He'd drawn a simple diagram on a single sheet of paper. It was a very effective summary of my talk.

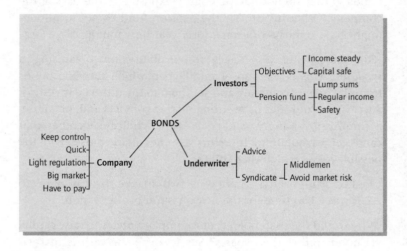

Day 2, 5.45pm – Broadgate, London

I thought back to Anisa's threats at St Pancras. In the coming weeks I had work trips planned to the US, Mexico and Hong Kong and was looking forward to diving in Thailand. At least two of those places needed visas. Since my clients in the US, Middle East and Asia arranged transport for me, they would need to see my passport upfront. It was slowly dawning on me that Anisa was in a strong position.

My mind buzzed with everything that had happened since I boarded that train to Paris. The permutations were endless. Why – and how – had Guy Abercrombie disappeared? Was Conrad a harmless old show-off or someone with more sinister aims? What were the chances that Anisa Chabbra would sit opposite me?

And what, exactly, was the nature of the government agency she worked for?

The more I thought about what was happening to me, the more crucial the Cal-Pan report became. I'd read it from cover to cover three times that morning. But I still couldn't work out what the company was planning.

7

Very interesting, Mr Bond

Jerry once came back from a meeting with HR and informed us that he had been told to brush up his appraisal techniques. 'They've told me that every negative comment has to be preceded by some positive news.'

Jerry looked out of the window. 'What a beautiful day,' he said. And then he looked at Jonathan Spurrier. 'And you are the biggest idiot that ever walked across the earth.'

By now Jerry's workforce was thirty-strong and we all laughed. But I was starting to feel sorry for Jonathan. Jerry's humour often crossed into bullying. His latest torture was the Rapid Fire Round. At the end of each day Jerry would pick someone at random. They were given an evening to prepare a topic. The next morning they had to stand up in front of the whole department while Jerry fired off questions. It was an ordeal all of us had to suffer but Jonathan was chosen more often than the rest of us put together.

One morning Jerry, his clothes reeking of cigarette smoke and gin, made Jonathan stand up and tell us what he knew about bonds.

The old principle/principal trade-off

'A bond is a debt obligation.'

'What does that mean?' Jerry interrupted.

'It's like an IOU. A company or government issues a bond. It promises to pay the investor interest payments and to pay back the amount of the loan.'

'When?'

'On dates set out in a contract.'

'What do investors call these interest payments that flow from a bond?'

'Coupons.'

'Why?'

'Because the bond used to be a big piece of paper. Investors tore off a coupon every six months and exchanged it for cash at a bank.'

Jonathan was doing well. It grieved me to see that Jonathan's confidence made Jerry more aggressive.

'What happens at the end of the bond's life?'

'The bond matures.'

'And?'

'The principal is paid back to the investor.'

'What's that?'

'The principal is the original value of the bond. If you paid £100 for the bond ten years ago, the company has to pay you back £100 on maturity.'

'What's maturity?'

'It's the life of a bond. Some bonds last for a year, some last for forty. Five- and ten-year bonds are common.'

Jonathan certainly knew the terminology. Perhaps he was cleverer than he'd let on.

'Anything you'd care to add?' There was a sneer in Jerry's voice.

Jonathan took a deep breath and stared straight into Jerry's face. 'A firm issuing bonds gets in cash but doesn't give away any control. Bondholders can't tell you how to run your company, no matter how many bonds in the company they hold.' I was amazed by Jonathan's concise explanation of company law. 'Shares are the opposite. Once someone has more than half of your share capital they can pretty much do anything they like. They own the majority of the company, so they can choose to expand into Brazil, open a factory in India or sell your Chinese division to the highest bidder. And get rid of the original owners any time they like.'

I'd always believed that the Rapid Fire Round had been designed by Jerry to remind us that Jerry was boss. But this time I was actually learning a lot. I looked around to see that everyone else was paying full attention. Jerry's face, it was fair to say, was not a picture of happiness.

'Who are the biggest buyers of bonds?' Jerry demanded. I looked at Perrine. She was staring at Jonathan – stupid, oafish Jonathan Spurrier – with admiration. And he was looking right back at her, enjoying his moment in the limelight.

'Institutional investors like asset management firms and insurance companies. Pension funds seem to love them.'

'Why?'

'Pension funds know that in thirty years their investors will retire. So they go for bonds of the same maturity. They get back the principal at the same time they need to make lump sum payments to their pensioners.'

'Why don't they choose equities instead?'

The name's Safety

'Equities pay dividends but they aren't guaranteed. If a company has a terrible year they won't have any profit to pay the dividend. And it may be that management want to keep profits to re-invest in the company. But the coupon is guaranteed. In good years or bad, the investor will get the coupon.'

❝ Equities pay dividends but they aren't guaranteed ❞

'So?'

'They get a safe, steady income and their capital is protected. If the company goes bust, the bond investors are higher up in the list of who gets paid. It's perfect for investors who can't risk their money. Their money is safe and their income is guaranteed, as long as the company remains solvent.'

'What else is wrong about equities for risk-averse investors?'

'A company doesn't have a maturity date. It could be like IBM and outlive us all. Or it could go bust tomorrow. Either way, there's no fixed maturity. That means no guarantee that investors get back their original investment.'

'But if bonds are so safe, why did so many of them collapse in value during the last financial crisis?'

'Too many companies issued too many bonds at a time when the economy was already collapsing. They weren't making enough money to pay the coupons, let alone the principal repayment. Greed moved the bonds from low risk/low return to high risk/low return. As first one company, and then another, failed to pay their debts, investors cut their losses and sold them.'

He was good. Hell would freeze over before Jerry would concede that Jonathan Spurrier was a bond expert. But I was certainly impressed.

Ratings measure risk – usually

That evening Perrine and I shared the lift down. She looked worried. Jerry had told her she'd been selected for the Rapid Fire Round tomorrow morning. He'd given her advance warning that the subject was bond ratings.

'How much do you know about ratings?'

'Not enough,' she admitted.

'I bet I can teach you about them before we get across the bridge.'

'Go on.'

'The most commonly used ratings system comes from Standard & Poor's. Anything rated between AAA and BBB is an investment-grade bond. That means any investment fund can buy it. At the top of the pile you've got a bond rated AAA, which is pronounced "triple A". That means it's regarded as being risk-free.'

'What company on earth is risk-free?'

'None of them, these days. But governments can be very safe, especially if the country they run is well-developed and highly profitable. The government issues the bond and uses tax money to pay off the interest. People believe that the UK government can never go bust.'

'But countries do go bust, don't they? What happens to a country's bonds when it has financial problems?'

'The rating is cut and the price will fall. Some investors may choose to cut their losses, and others might see it as a chance to buy. It's risk and return in action.

'A rating is meant to sum up all the good things and bad things about a company or a government. It's a simple way to show the risk of a bond. The job of a credit analyst is to work out the riskiness of a bond, so investors don't have to wade through reams of financial statements and complicated cash flow projections. The rating is a single measure that sums up all their research.'

But we were out of time. I handed her this piece of paper.

---

fast facts

Things you need to know about credit rating agencies

Credit rating agencies are a vital part of the financial world. They rate governments and companies on the likelihood that they will pay interest and the principal back to the lender.

A rating is a **credit score for a company.** Think about the factors that lenders take into account when you apply for a mortgage or a

▶ credit card. What is your income, how big are your existing debts, have you been approved by another company? It's the same for a company.

Agencies suffer from a **conflict of interest** because of the way they make money. They charge companies for a rating, and companies are happy to pay because it's pretty impossible to raise bond finance without one. There's a suspicion that agencies may have been blinded by corporate relationships.

(The agencies were widely criticised for the poor quality of their ratings during the collapse of the financial markets in 2008. It was clear that many staff were **lacking in knowledge** when analysing complex bonds.)

Ratings represent an opinion at a single point of time and may rely on historical information. Professional investors use agency reports as the **first step in analysis** rather than the definitive last word.

'Thanks,' Perrine said. 'I owe you for this.'

My mind churned with jokey replies about obligations and debts. Thankfully the internal switch which monitored my worst attempts at finance-based humour had kicked in. I decided to say nothing.

'Perhaps I can get you a drink sometime in repayment.' Her words, not mine.

---

fast facts

We start with the **investment grade** bonds

AAA	The best-quality borrowers, reliable and stable
AA	Quality borrowers, a bit higher risk than AAA
A	Economic situation can affect finance
BBB	The lowest level of investment grade

And move into **junk** bonds

BB	Can be badly affected by changes in the economy
B	Looking bad
CCC	Extremely vulnerable
CC	Going ...
C	Going ...

Lastly, we have bonds that are **in default**

D	Gone

Day 2, 6.00pm – Old Street, London

Messages, messages, messages. My phone beeped and buzzed with emails, voicemails and texts. All of them came from Anisa.

Her instructions were to meet outside Old Street tube as soon as I was finished with the lawyers. She stood, scowling, by the entrance to one of the very select number of German bierkellers in the UK.

She handed me a list of the investments Guy Abercrombie was suspected of making.

'Look at these,' she ordered. 'And come back to me tomorrow with what you find.'

'I'll tell you what, Anisa. I'll research Guy Abercrombie's activities for you. But only if you promise not to tell any of my clients about your investigation.'

Anisa's face had hardened. She flicked a strand of hair away from her right eye and our eyes met. 'Do you really think you're in a position to bargain with me?' she asked.

'No. But I reckon you need my help as much as I need yours.'

'Work on this tonight,' Anisa said without breaking her gaze. 'Then I'll decide if your research is worth anything.'

8

Chinese walls come tumbling down

Jerry Witts loved to display his collection of deal toys. These are the trinkets that clients award bankers after a successful deal.

Jerry showed me a succession of tombstones, thick blocks of Lucite with the details of each deal encased in the middle. Some of the toys were a little more imaginative: carriage clocks in solid silver and a scale model of a Rolls Royce handcrafted in gold. Pride of place went to a rather arty platinum paperweight. That came from a grateful oligarch who had landed a state-owned mining company for 4 per cent of its true value.

But there were two deal toys that were always kept hidden from clients who visited his inner sanctum. Jerry would take the key he kept hidden in his desk drawer and unlock the simple safe he used for confidential papers. When he was feeling tired – and Jerry was looking more and more exhausted with each day that passed – Jerry would show me the pig and the truck.

The pig was so heavy I needed both hands to lift it. It had been made from melted-down coins. I could make out 50p pieces, pesetas, drachmas and francs. Worst of all, the pig had been painted bright pink by the currency-brokers who had made a fortune from turmoil in the markets.

'Why don't you throw that ugly thing away?' I asked Jerry.

'I can't. It's the eyes.'

The pink pig had staring eyes the size of tablespoons. Had the stress got to Jerry? Had he finally cracked? 'Do you think they are following you around the room?'

'No, you idiot. They're made of rhodium. They're worth a fortune!'

Deals on wheels

The second toy was much more interesting. Jerry never lifted it from its hiding place. It was a plastic toy rubbish truck, value about £4, with AFS scribbled in ballpoint on the driver's door. Inside the truck, in the section where rubbish was churned, was about £500 of roughly shredded bank notes. There was another scrawl on the truck's roof: *This represents all my money which you left on the table when you sold my company too cheaply.*

I raised an eyebrow and Jerry explained. 'AFS was one of a handful of companies in its rather specialised sector. If investors wanted to get access to the steady cash flows AFS produced they would have to pay a premium for its unique franchise. Stock turnover was constant and a steady stream of customers was guaranteed.'

'So what went wrong?'

'Nothing. We sold 100 per cent of the company at £1 a share. The owner made £240 million. In the next few weeks, the share price went up to £1.50. He was furious because he thought we should have sold his company for £360 million.'

'What was AFS?'

'Associated Funeral Services. When the bloody owner told me I'd wasted his once in a lifetime opportunity I thought he was joking. And then he said that his dreams of joining the super-rich were dead and buried. I laughed so hard I had to put the phone down. But he was serious. Hence the rubbish truck.'

Such was the difference between success and failure. A big fat rhodium-embellished pig or a rude message scribbled on the side of a child's toy by a pissed-off client.

Sales and profits are recorded in a firm's income statement

Jerry chose the morning after the firm's summer ball to teach me how to look at a company's income statement. (Jerry preferred to call it the P&L, short for *profit and loss*.) 'Turnover records all the products and services a company has sold during a year. It totals the sales made by the company. Expenses include staff, technology, marketing spend and office running costs. The company will also have interest expenses if it has borrowed money during the year. And it will have to pay tax, which we regard as a running cost, just like any other cost.'

Jerry pulled out the accounts of Golden Orchid, a Japanese company he was analysing. All the figures were in millions of yen and started to swim across the page in front of me. The company sold goods worth ¥180,000 but incurred costs of ¥60,000. This meant that the profit before tax was ¥120,000 (the ¥180,000 minus the ¥60,000). The company had to pay ¥20,000 in tax.

Jerry looked at my hung-over face. 'Are you paying attention, student?'

I nodded but Jerry didn't appear convinced. He decided to revert to his preferred teaching technique – sarcasm.

'The profit before tax was ¥120,000 and tax was ¥20,000. Can you put your highly tuned super-computer of a brain to work and tell me what was the profit after tax?'

I spluttered out the answer. '¥100,000.'

'Great work, mastermind. Glad to see your university education hasn't been wasted.'

Income statement		Yen (m)
A	Turnover	180,000
B	Costs	− 60,000
C = A−B	Profit before tax	120,000
D	Tax	− 20,000
E = C−D	Profit after tax	100,000

A firm can pay profit out as dividend or keep it within the company

Jerry then showed me how Golden Orchid split its profit after tax. ¥30,000 was paid out in dividends, leaving ¥70,000 to be retained within the company.

'What's vital to know is that dividends are not an expense. A dividend payment is a way for the management to split the profit after tax. It's apportioned between *dividends* (money which leaves the company and is paid to its shareholders) and *retained profits* (money which is kept within the company and added to its capital).'

Apportioning profit	Yen (m)
E Profit after tax	100,000
F Total dividend	30,000
G Profit retained	70,000

Front running

Jerry was king of the aphorism. 'Problems are merely opportunities prohibited by the regulators' was a typical gnomic utterance.

❝ Problems are merely opportunities prohibited by the regulators ❞

I'd been with Saiwai for three years before Jerry Witts told me about some of the problems with the organisation of the bank. He made it clear that the problems were immensely profitable for his team of proprietary traders.

'What are proprietary traders?'

'Traders who do deals on the bank's behalf. They use Saiwai's capital to make a profit for Saiwai.'

'Got it.'

'Look at our oil guys. Imagine they have client orders to buy one billion barrels and there are no sell orders in the whole market. So demand is going to push up the price of oil. There's no law to stop my prop traders from buying oil for Saiwai's own account. But if we do it ever so slightly before we fulfil our client order we can be 99 per cent certain that we'll make a gain. And that's called *front running*.'

'I must stress,' continued Jerry as he stared at a trader's screen, 'that front running is illegal. It's also highly profitable, difficult to detect and hard to prove. Weigh it up. Big bonus against tiny risk. You'd be tempted, wouldn't you?'

I drew my own conclusions.

During one of the tube strikes that were a feature of the summer of 1989 in London, Jerry would accept no slacking. This was an age when working from home was an impossible dream. I always remember Jonathan Spurrier rollerblading ten miles from his Wimbledon flat to the office. His mighty effort to work with the team was not an unqualified success, however. He had failed to bring in a change of clothes the day before. The stink from his sweatshirt filled the floor.

Jonathan Spurrier's continued employment at Saiwai puzzled Perrine. 'It's like a cretin paradox,' she told me one night over a pizza at hers. This time I didn't feel the need to correct her.

Private equity

Jerry arranged to meet me at The Blackfriars the following lunchtime. 'I want to talk to you about private equity,' was all he said.

'Private equity experts typically buy businesses that are mature. They like companies that have predictable revenues and very solid cash flows. Think of a chain of pubs. They'll look for a strong brand, with high recognition amongst its customers. It should also be backed up by physical assets, including the pubs, distribution centres and a head office.'

Jerry emptied half of his pint glass in a single gulp. 'Private equity is about the stable and steady, not the fast-growing and volatile. A private equity fund invests in large companies which are normally listed on the stock exchange. It takes them away from the gaze of public attention by turning them private. This removes the need for short-term shareholder satisfaction.

'Private equity funds are often criticised for being vultures. They counteract this with claims that they create value by running businesses more efficiently. And they put their money where their mouths are by investing with their own money.

'I want to show you how Saiwai helps the funds. But first …' Jerry rattled his empty glass in front of my face.

'Same again?' I asked.

'Do you really need to ask?'

---

case study

Every mistake imaginable

EMI was sold to Terra Firma, a British private equity firm, in November 2007. It was the start of a nightmare for both the music label and its new owners.

Terra Firma's main man, Guy Hands, proclaimed his bold plan. EMI was to be transformed into the leading music company of the twenty-first century. Terra Firma's turnarounds of Odeon Cinemas and the William Hill chain of betting shops had been astounding. Hands wanted multiple rights deals, whereby EMI would take a cut of an artist's touring revenues and merchandise sales. Taking EMI private would enable Hands to restructure and invest without reporting to shareholders every six months.

Almost immediately he cut 2,000 jobs, and that's when his problems began. The music industry is like no other. Even good record companies find it hard to make money in the post-Napster world. EMI had been loss-making for years. It was small in comparison to the sector's major players – Universal and Sony BMG. The artists, and those who discovered them, were revered. Hidden cash payments for 'fruit and flowers' – that's 'drugs' if you can't crack codes – were not unheard of (see www.guardian.co.uk/business/2011/oct/28/emi-sold-russian-billionaire).

Artists soon rebelled against the new owners. Hands' PR team responded by leaking stories to music and finance journalists about the excessive demands of EMI's spoiled artists. Radiohead, who were especially vocal about the place of private equity in the music business, were distraught to read that they had asked for £3 million for their next album. Mind you, they're not the happiest bunch at the best of times.

Hands lost the Rolling Stones and Queen to rival labels. You can think of these acts as the equivalent of the value stocks you encountered in Chapter 5: they won't trouble the top of the charts but they will produce a steady stream of cash flow. The financial crisis made it impossible for Terra Firma to secure the cheap financing it needed. Hands' plans collapsed in a storm of lawsuits and backbiting. And two of the oddest industries in the world – music and finance – once again failed to achieve harmony.

case study

Four weird music and investment crossovers

Sting lost £4.8 million after trusting his royalties to notorious show-business accountant Keith Moore. Moore funnelled the money into a series of increasingly desperate business ventures, including a plan to turn Russian military planes into passenger jumbos. At the other end of the ecological scale, Moore also put Sting's money into an environmentally friendly gearbox.

The Rolling Stones. Microsoft paid at least $5 million to license *Start Me Up* to announce Windows 95. Sadly, no money was left to teach Bill Gates to dance.

U2. The investment arm of the Irish rock behemoth has always been famous for its record of terrible investments. All that is set to change, however, because of its holding in Facebook.

Leonard Cohen. The Canadian singer and poet was swindled out of his $5 million retirement fund by unscrupulous management. Cohen, a Buddhist, sanguinely noted that news of the loss was 'enough to put a dent in one's mood'.

EBIT doh!

I came back from the bar to find Jerry had a file open in front of him. It was stamped *Golden Orchid – Private and Confidential*. He pulled out a printout as ash tumbled from his cigarette. A key fell from his trouser pocket. I recognised it as the key to his office safe.

'Why haven't you left the key in your office?' I asked.

'No reason,' he snapped back. 'Pay attention. You need to concentrate on EBIT.'

'What's that?'

'It's the *earnings* a company makes *before* it pays out *interest or tax*. Sometimes it's known as *operating profit*.'

'Why?'

'Because, brains, it's the profit the company makes from its operations. It hasn't yet paid out any money to pay its debt and it hasn't yet paid any money out in the form of tax.'

'So what?'

'Is it National Thick Day today? I hope your love-life isn't giving you problems.'

I said nothing, Jerry took a pull on his new pint and continued. 'It's smart to assess a company before interest and tax distort its operational performance. Look at Golden Orchid.'

Income statement	Yen (m)
Turnover	180,000
Costs	− 60,000
EBIT	120,000

I did a quick mental calculation. At the operating level Golden Orchid was incredibly profitable. Its costs were only one-third of its income. Its operating margin was 66.7 per cent (120,000 divided by 180,000), which was very wide.

'Golden Orchid is currently financed just by its shareholders. It doesn't have any borrowings. Is that a good or a bad thing?'

'Good, I guess. They don't have to pay any interest so there is more profit.'

'Wrong answer. We actually want Golden Orchid to pay interest so it reduces profit.'

'Why? Surely that makes the company more risky?'

Jerry smiled. 'Welcome, young man, to the world of investment banking.' He flourished another spreadsheet. 'This is Golden Orchid at the moment. Take a glance and tell me what you see.'

Income statement	Yen (m)
Turnover	180,000
Costs	− 60,000
EBIT	120,000
Interest paid	0
Profit before tax	120,000
Tax @ 25%	− 30,000
Profit after tax	90,000
Dividends paid	− 40,000
Profit retained	50,000

'The company pays no interest, so its profit before tax is exactly the same as its EBIT. It pays ¥30,000 in tax. It gives ¥40,000 to shareholders and retains ¥50,000.'

'Fine. Now look at my proposal. Instead of paying ¥40,000 to shareholders we pay ¥40,000 to bondholders. What changes because Golden Orchid has borrowed money?'

Income statement	Yen (m)
Turnover	180,000
Costs	−60,000
EBIT	120,000
Interest paid	−40,000
Profit before tax	80,000
Tax @ 25%	−20,000
Profit after tax	60,000
Dividends paid	0
Profit retained	60,000

'The profit is lower because Golden Orchid pays ¥40,000 in interest. Profit before tax falls, and this means the tax is now ¥20,000 not ¥30,000.'

'OK, I get that.'

'Now here's the clever bit. Look at the profit retained. It's gone up from ¥50,000 to ¥60,000. We've made an extra ¥10,000 profit for the shareholders.'

'How?'

'The business at the operating level – which is what EBIT shows – hasn't changed at all. But Saiwai has created ¥10,000 of extra value by changing the funding from equity to debt. Interest expense is a cost of running the business. It's a tax-deductible expense, just like your pitiful salary or my huge bonus. Or even the electricity and light we spend on keeping Perrine's desk lit up. By the way, how is it going with her?'

I marvelled at just how quickly office gossip spreads. It seemed that even people who couldn't stand the sight of each other spent whole lunchtimes dissecting my love-life. Or lack of it.

Jerry continued. 'It's quite common for private equity funds to take over the running of a business, put in new management and take on more debt. In a way, this switches the risk from the equity investors to the bank that is lending them the money.'

'So our job is to encourage businesses to borrow as much money as they can.'

'Almost right.'

'What do you mean?'

'Not our job. Your job.'

Jerry tried to stagger out of the pub but he couldn't open the door. His precious briefcase fell on the floor.

'Take this case for me and lock it in my safe. And for the love of God please get me a taxi.'

'Sure. But how can I open the safe?'

Jerry fumbled in his pockets and handed me the key.

'Say nothing to nobody,' he warned. 'Even the Chinese walls at Saiwai have ears!'

Behind the Chinese walls

A Chinese wall is a structure which stops information flow between different departments at an investment bank. But the walls at Saiwai were extremely porous.

The mergers and acquisitions department (M&A) provided finance for Atkins, a high-end but rather staid department store. The board of Atkins consisted of three bickering family members – William, Thomas and Patrick – and a selection of hand-picked yes-men and has-beens. They were planning to buy and rebrand Waugh Brothers, a chain of discount retailers.

Atkins had a record of poor acquisitions and terrible cost controls. Its management were disorganised and lazy. By contrast, Waugh Brothers was run by two sharp lads from Preston who'd fought for every penny during a meteoric business career. And they had three other offers from potential buyers on the desk.

It didn't take a genius to work out that a bidding frenzy would develop for Waugh Brothers. Rollerblading Jonathan Spurrier – who certainly wasn't a genius – reckoned that Atkins would not lose face and back out of the deal even if it meant over-paying. Knowledge about the deal was secret and restricted. Jerry kept a file with all the sensitive information on the Atkins deal in his safe.

Spurrier didn't trust his memory and jotted down the main gist of the deal – *Short Atkins, Go Long Waugh* – on a scrap of paper. He folded the paper into his jacket pocket and rewarded himself with a quick drink in Saiwai's local pub, The Blackfriars.

Three hours later and the scrap of paper was found by Rosa Stoddard, an equities trader who specialised in UK retail. She bought as many Waugh Brothers shares as she could find from investors who didn't know the bids were coming. She shorted Atkins shares with counterparties who had no idea another disastrous acquisition was about to be approved.

> **❝ The temptation to cheat when all this valuable info is flying about is strong ❞**

The temptation to cheat when all this valuable info is flying about is strong. I thought back to poor Brenda Leckie, whose job was to enforce barriers between departments. Jerry's game with the heating in her office demonstrated how little he valued the compliance department.

Traders were barred from the M&A department, and M&A bankers found that their swipes couldn't open the glass and chrome portals to the trading floor. But real life tends to get in the way of the best intentions of compliance. These people all work for the same firm, go to the same gym and share many of the same friends. They'll talk about work together, because that's what people do.

How effective are Chinese walls? Not at all, if truth were told, but let's keep up the pretence, eh?

I'd been under Jerry Witts' wings for five years. His erratic behaviour was well known amongst clients and contacts. A headhunter called me and asked, 'What the devil are you doing with that liability? Why not dip a toe in the interview pool and see if anyone gets wet.' Which was the head-hunter's way of telling me he'd arranged an interview for me at APX, a competitor bank.

One Friday afternoon I met with the Automaton. After thirty seconds with him I knew I could never work for APX. He seemed to be reading from a script about how great it was to work at APX, how selective they were in choosing people, how driven the employees needed to be to impress the directors.

The room fell silent and I asked a question to fill the dead air. 'Could you give me an example of the dedication you're looking for?'

'Yes. I have only seen my son twice in the last two weeks.'

'How old is he?' I wasn't interested, but I was desperate to find anything to talk about.

'He's two weeks old.'

That was enough for me.

I had begun to see burnout in people who'd spent only a few years in finance. Everybody I met was making more than 99 per cent of the working population and yet they suffered a constant, gnawing dissatisfaction. Most people realise that there's more to life, and take a career break. They do yoga in Atsitsa, scuba diving in Cozumel, trekking in Nepal. If they take more than three months off, they will never take a job in investment finance seriously.

Some, though, get to thirty and take the opposite route. When they realise that there are still people richer than them in the world, they go mad with envy. Their solution is to work harder, and longer, and with more drive and purpose, until they are effectively living in the office and using their home as a place to sleep and store clothes. They're the ones who are happy to work fifteen hours a day and give up their weekends to be in the office. Any family and friends they once had are strangers to them now. And money – instead of being the way to freedom – becomes its own designer-labelled trap.

I shook hands with the Automaton and mumbled something about keeping my options open. He led me down to reception. But through the sparkling glass and shiny aluminium of APX's offices I saw the reflection of a head I recognised. A closer look proved it was Jonathan Spurrier.

My first thought was perhaps Jonathan was interviewing as well. Then I noticed his jacket was off and his tie was at half-mast. At least twenty people were listening to him. Why? Jonathan Spurrier was delivering a presentation to a rival bank!

I pretended my shoelace was undone so that the Automaton had to stop. I bent down and saw the flipchart. I made out the words *Atkins* and *Waugh*. I rushed back to Saiwai in a cab. Jerry couldn't be found. It was Friday evening, after all, and he'd be legless in The Blackfriars by now.

I did what I did that night out of loyalty to Jerry Witts. Despite what was to happen, I still to this day believe I acted honestly.

I had the key to Jerry's stupid collection of toys and I thought he was too drunk to move, let alone do anything else more energetic. It was down to me – and me alone – to save Saiwai from a massive hit. I was certain that APX knew about the deal. They had the resources to put huge amounts of money behind their trade. Saiwai, a small player, would be sunk by the money APX was betting against us. Jerry was certain to lose his job. The Atkins family would sue Saiwai for millions which it simply didn't have. Corporate insolvency was a real possibility.

I had to make sure my fears were grounded in reality before I made any allegations against Jonathan Spurrier. I pretended to work until the floor had emptied and the coast was clear. One of Jerry's sayings was that *dirty work is best done out in the open*. So I strolled into the office, as if I had left my pen on his desk, and shut the door behind me.

I slipped the key into the safe. There was no sign of the Atkins file. Then I heard the footsteps. I could tell straightaway that they didn't belong to a stray post boy or a random cleaner. Unless the post boy could afford handmade brogues and the cleaning lady dusted the offices in stilettos.

I ducked down under Jerry's desk a second before the door opened. The footsteps belonged to Jerry and Perrine. They tumbled drunkenly in, knocking over a chair and a pot plant. The contents of his desk cascaded to the floor. Jerry's Montblanc landed an inch in front of my nose.

Jerry bent down to pick it up. 'What in God's name are you doing down there?' he thundered.

With a great deal of stammering I explained about the Atkins file and the interview at APX. And then I told them about Jonathan Spurrier. 'He's a double agent, Jerry. He's taking our information and selling it to APX. It's like *Tinker, Tailor, Soldier, Spy* and Jonathan Spurrier is the mole.'

Jerry looked up at me and suddenly the drunkenness seemed to disappear. 'I've known for a year that Jonathan has been visiting our competitors.'

'Why haven't you done anything about it?'

'Because Jonathan isn't a double agent. He's a triple agent. He gives fake information to APX, and then tells me what they're working on. Some of our best tips have come from him. He has to make himself look as thick as a plank here, but he's my smartest operator.'

'But it's illegal to trade on that kind of information. Even if you make a huge profit for the bank, the board will sack you as soon as they find out.'

'The board will never find out what I'm doing. That is, unless you tell them. You see, whizzkid, the profits I make all come to me. I'm doing the trades from my own personal account. I really doubt if compliance will go all the way to Zurich to hunt it down.'

Jerry looked at Perrine and smiled through gritted teeth. 'What should we do with him? He'll be captured on security videos opening the safe and hiding under the desk. It won't look good.'

Perrine said nothing. Her presence emboldened me to take a risk. I decided to return the threat. 'I'm sure APX have security cameras as well, Jerry. Shall I pop round to see how clear their images of Jonathan are?'

He asked Perrine to leave. We sat facing each other for the first time since that fateful interview.

'Let me do a deal with you, young man. You need to leave work immediately. Tell people you've got burned out or there's a death in the family. If you keep silent, I will continue to pay you a salary to an untraceable account. You're always banging on about travel. Pack up your rucksack and clear off to see the world. You can take *la belle dame sans merci* with you.'

I nodded. It was the best offer I had ever had in my life. A great salary, in a tax-free account, without having to do any work. It was impossible to refuse.

'There's just one proviso,' Jerry said. 'I'm allowed to call you three times to ask for help. You can't refuse me when I get in touch.'

'Agreed.' And, weirdly, we shook hands like we were agreeing a sale.

'Deal,' we both said.

Day 2, 8.00pm – Marylebone, London

The day was turning into a problem.

I had made no progress on finding out about Guy Abercrombie's whereabouts or his nefarious activities. I dug out the Cal-Pan report and sneaked another peek. There was a list of rare and precious metals on page 5. I didn't recognise any of them except for rhodium. I called the one person I knew who might be able to help and arranged to meet her early the next morning.

I had also agreed to do a radio interview with Karl Honey, an unreliable contact of mine who sometimes freelanced for the BBC. We met in Coco Momo, a bar in Marylebone High Street, and he was his normal half-hour late.

'You're looking smart, Karl.' It was the first time I'd seen him clean-shaven. In fact, he was positively groomed. Above the smell of cocktails and Guinness I detected aftershave. I had always had doubts about Karl's personal cleanliness and so today was a revelation.

'There's a new woman in my life, that's why. I've had to smarten up. Anyway, down to business. Have you heard, mate, about this thing called Cal-Pan?'

'No,' I lied, stuffing the Cal-Pan report back into my case. 'What is it?'

'Rumour on the street is that they're planning to build a railway.' Karl Honey sniffed, then gulped down most of his pint of lager.

'Wow. Cutting-edge stuff. They'll be branching out into fax machines next.'

'Listen, it's a railway across central America. To transport freight from the Pacific to the Atlantic.'

'So?'

'It'll be cheaper and quicker than the Panama Canal, IMHO. The chap who told me said it'll be a bonanza.'

'Who was the chap who told you?'

'Hold on a sec, I've got it here.' Karl fumbled into his bag and pulled out a scrappy notepad. 'That's right. Abercrombie. Guy Abercrombie. You ever heard of him?'

He stared at me for an answer but I said nothing. 'What's up, mate. You look like you've seen a ghost.'

part

three

You can always get what you want

9

The meek shall inherit the mineral rights

Day 3, 8.00am – Corpus Christi College, Cambridge

'Greetings, Whizzkid.'

Professor Lena Gallis called me by a nickname I hadn't heard for years. Her study was typical Cambridge: books crammed into rickety shelves and stiff card invitations on the marble mantelpiece. Lena started poring over her manuscripts at six in the morning to make the best of the light.

College gossip-mongers whispered that Lena had recruited students for the British secret services. There were rumours of dark deeds she'd committed in her native Latvia after the Russian occupation. I'd always hoped that one day she'd send me to some glamorous hotbed of spying – Cairo, for example, or Moscow. Sadly, she'd never offered me anything more exciting than biscuits and a glass of college sherry.

'You look tired,' she said. 'Working too hard?'

'No. I'm just preoccupied. I've got some questions about the commodity markets.'

'What do you want to know?'

'Everything.'

'How long have you got?'

'Ten minutes.'

Essential ingredients – rice, wheat and oil

Lena took a deep breath, steepled her hands together and leaned forward. It was a familiar pose from our supervisions so many years before. 'I'd better begin. The commodity market splits neatly into two parts. There's trading in the *physical commodities*, such as oil and wheat and orange juice. And then there are the *derivatives* which are based on these physical commodities.

'Scholars have uncovered proof that derivatives – in particular, forwards – have been used for centuries.' Lena was in full flow. 'The Dojima Rice Exchange in Osaka first opened for business in 1710. Or 1730 or 1693, no one's really sure because of missing records and the use of different calendars. A rice farmer would sell his harvest to a monastery chef before it had finished growing. Why? First, the farmer needed money to rent the land or buy seed or pay for labour. Any cash received early would also be welcome.

'The second advantage, and probably the most important thing from the farmer's perspective, was that he was guaranteed a buyer who would take his rice at a fixed price. You see, that's how a *forward* works. The buyer and the seller of a commodity agree on a price today, but the goods will change hands at a specified date in the future.'

I leaned forward to ask a question. 'Why did the monastery chef use the forward?'

'He needed to be sure that he would have rice to feed the monks. And he was also interested in the certainty of price. If rice prices suddenly spiked because of a bad harvest, the chef would have to pay loads more to feed his samurai. So forwards were always about safety. They were a way for the two people in the contract to avoid risk.'

Lena suddenly switched from talking about counterparty trades to the birth of the major commodity marketplaces.

'We can really trace modern commodity markets to the American Midwest during the boom years of the 1840s. Wheat farmers in the Prairie belt needed a place to meet buyers from the fast-growing cities of the East Coast. The railroads brought buyers and sellers to Chicago, and an informal exchange built around saloons and hotels became more formalised. People began dealing on the *spot market*, exchanging wheat for cash there and then. Soon they would be buying futures as well.'

'Have you heard of these, Lena?' I handed her a copy of the Cal-Pan list. What were antimony and columbite-tantalite and neodymium? What on earth was rhodium?

'Interesting,' she said. Lena balanced her glasses on the bridge of her nose. Her face screwed up in concentration. 'Very interesting.'

'What?' I felt that at last I was making progress.

'That I've never heard of any of these things!' Lena was off again, giving me precisely detailed but not particularly up-to-date information. 'For thousands of years people were perfectly happy to trade physical commodities. The Sogdians established the Silk Route, and the Romans and the Greeks set up a network of ports that criss-crossed the Mediterranean.'

I watched dust twisting in a column of sunlight as Lena talked about tokens and money, olive oil and tin. And gold, the most important commodity ever discovered. Our meeting ended with her familiar joke about my former college across the road from Corpus Christi. 'Upstart college', she spluttered in mock indignation. 'Only been around since 1473!'

---

case study

Oil is the world's most influential commodity

The supply of oil is tightly controlled by OPEC, an organisation of twelve developing countries. Its influence is not total, however, because Russia, the US and other energy-producers are not members. OPEC members own 79 per cent of the known current oil reserves in the world. (OPEC was one of my clients. They're lovely people, but their offices in Vienna are strangely under-heated.)

> ▶ Oil is a commodity traded by thousands of speculators
> across the world. Its price doubled in the first six months
> of 2008, then dropped by two-thirds in the last half of the
> year. Land-based reserves are dwindling and recent disasters
> demonstrate how difficult it is to safely drill offshore. Demand
> fluctuates swiftly and often. Economic growth demands fuel
> for production and distribution. Tensions in the Middle East
> or the illness of a Venezuelan president will change oil's
> price. Speculators may love volatility, but manufacturers and
> motorists certainly don't.
>
> **Film fact** – *The World Is Not Enough* was the nineteenth
> James Bond movie. Its razor-thin plot concerns a scam to
> increase oil prices by exploding a nuclear bomb in the waters
> of Istanbul. Fans of bad acting will be delighted by Goldie's
> appearance as a villain.

I walked down King's Parade towards Trinity College, thinking how different my teaching style was from Lena's. I'm always up against the clock with my courses, getting as much knowledge across as possible in the shortest available time. My examples have to be up-to-date and have a practical application. The directors who pay me to teach their staff are always looking for an immediate return on their investment.

Take the Americans I had to teach in three days' time. Their job is to settle trades, and they work in the middle office. They sit between the traders in the front office, and the back office which analyses whether a trade has been profitable or not. They are shouted at by traders during the working day and then spend most of the evening getting grief from accountants and auditors.

The case studies I design for them have to be quick and direct. Like this one, on sausages.

The best way to meet your sausage meat needs

You are a sausage manufacturer, famed for your pork sausages. You always experience a surge in demand when the barbecue season starts in three months' time. What three choices do you have now? And what are the pros and cons of each choice?

Choice 1 – Buy now and store

You have guaranteed your raw materials and you know the price. You'll have to pay for storage and wastage, though. The big drawback is that the price may be lower in the future.

Choice 2 – Buy in the spot market in three months

You can wait three months and buy the sausage meat on the day you need it. You hand over the cash, and take the meat back to your factory.

This strategy exposes you to two big risks. You may not be able to find enough sausage meat and the price may have risen because of factors you didn't predict.

Choice 3 – Use a forward contract

You agree with the pig farmer to buy a certain weight and quality of sausage meat three months down the line.

The forward contract fixes a price for your raw materials and guarantees your delivery. The big disadvantage is that you won't benefit if the price of pork drops in the next three months. You won't be able to buy at the cheaper market price.

But you are a sausage producer, not a pig trader. You should stick to the business you know and choose certainty of price over risk-taking.

Day 3, 8.30am – Cambridge Market

The phone rang.

Anisa sounded like she was in a wind tunnel. 'I need to ask you a question.'

'Another one?' I said it as a joke, but even I noticed the desperation in my voice.

'I don't remember setting a limit when you agreed to the deal that saved your hide.'

'OK. What is it?'

'What's shorting?'

'Shorting is the opposite of buying. It gives you a profit when the investment falls in price.' The line went quiet as I thought of another explanation. 'Imagine you're betting on a horse race.'

'Yep.'

'But you make money only if your horse finishes last.'

'So I make money from failure.'

'Yes. You make money by predicting the direction of a market or an investment. And the more the horse fails, the more cash you make.'

'So I want my horse to fall over at the first fence.'

'Ideally you want it to die the moment the starter fires his gun.'

'OK. I've got it. I'll need some more details later.'

'Why?'

It was Anisa's turn to be elusive. 'I've got an idea that's pure gold' was all she said before the line went dead.

Why do people buy gold?

I've always regarded gold as simultaneously valuable and a bit useless. It's great for jewellery and really good for your fillings, but aside from these things it doesn't have a huge number of practical uses. And yet most cultures are full of stories about gold. Think of *Goldfinger* and *The Treasure of the Sierra Madre*, King Midas and El Dorado.

For centuries gold has been a trusted form of payment. But it still retains a mystical, mythical allure that sausage meat will never have. All the emperors in the world and the kings of ancient kingdoms have been desperate to get gold, never lorry loads of edible palm oil.

Gold is the ultimate defensive investment during times of crisis. Shares and bonds normally perform well in stable economic and political environments. As soon as you have turmoil, bad harvests, threats of war, disease – all the horsemen of the economic apocalypse – the financial markets tumble. Investors don't trust equities because they become too volatile. Bonds lose their appeal because governments may refuse to pay coupons or, in the worst case, the principal. Gold is what investors turn to when they are frightened.

> **66 Gold is what investors turn to when they are frightened 99**

Gold is a fantastic way to avoid the pernicious impact of inflation. If interest rates are very low and inflation creeps above them, then holding cash will actually lead to a real loss. When interest rates are low, gold prices normally go up. In recent years, the nature of gold as an investment has changed. Investors in the financial markets now see gold as a way to make some serious returns and not just as a defensive play. Huge demand for gold jewellery has come from two of the largest emerging middle classes in the world at the moment – India and China.

Gold is not like cotton or soya beans because there's a finite supply. Once it's all mined, that's it. It's not possible to grow or produce any more. But it sticks around and it doesn't go off, like so many gallons of frozen orange juice.

All that glitters ...? Five facts about gold

All the gold that's been **mined** since the very beginning of civilisation would comfortably fit under the Eiffel Tower. The vast majority of all that gold is still in human hands.

Some scientists estimate there's 15,000 tonnes of gold swilling around at the bottom of the world's **oceans**.

The current **production** of gold is around 2,500 tonnes every year.

Each year 500 tonnes of gold is **added** to the pile bought and sold by investors.

Gold is used for jewellery, dentistry and some industrial processes. People have a much greater **emotional response** to gold than to silver, platinum or those flowers men buy from garages on Valentine's Day.

Price is where supply shakes hands with demand

How is a commodity priced? How, indeed, is any asset priced?

Waiting for the train, I formulated some answers, based on one of the great classics of English literature. In Thomas Hardy's *The Mayor of Casterbridge* the price of commodities has a direct connection to the destinies of the two major characters.

Michael Henchard is a powerful wheat merchant. Normally, demand for wheat runs at 10,000 bushels. Henchard is convinced that the harvest will be bad, and so buys wheat when it is trading at 5 shillings a bushel.

Increased demand pushes up prices

Henchard's buying spree increases the total demand for wheat from 10,000 to 15,000 bushels. But the supply of wheat cannot be increased overnight, so the more he buys the more he has to pay. Some merchants buy wheat from other towns to increase supply but they cannot get to 15,000. Henchard's last purchases are made at 8 shillings a bushel, which becomes the new market price.

Increased supply causes a fall in price

But Henchard's analysis – inspired by a visit to the local witch – is wrong. No sooner has he bought at 8 shillings, than the sun comes out over the golden fields. The abundant harvest leads to a massive increase in supply, so the price drops to 4 shillings a bushel.

A cut in supply pushes up the price

Henchard has to cut his losses and sells his bushels to his bitter rival, Donald Farfrae. What happens on the last day of the harvest is cruel. A deluge of rain destroys much of the corn and the market is spooked. The supply of wheat will only be 8,000 bushels. Wheat rises to 9 shillings a bushel, and Farfrae is heavily in the money.

The town's merchants scrabble desperately to buy wheat. Farfrae suddenly makes enough money to be the most important player in the market. Once the penniless newcomer, he has become the ideal candidate to replace the bankrupt Henchard as town mayor.

A modern-day Henchard would cover his position with a variety of futures. The modern-day Farfrae would probably have retired at 27, having made a vast fortune from his wheat hedge fund.

case study

Choc Fingers

In 2011 a hedge fund called Armajaro Holdings paid £658 million to buy a quarter of a million tons of cocoa beans. The purchase made by Anthony Ward, main man at the company, was enough to make 5.3 billion chocolate bars. Portrayed by the media as a bizarre mix of Willy Wonka and chocoholic Bond villain, Ward is, rather predictably, now known as *Choc Fingers*.

The beans were bought just as the price rose to its highest level since a boom in 1977. The 1970s boom coincided with me first receiving an income from a Saturday job, but economists consider it unlikely that my sweet tooth was enough to move the market. Which again shows how little economists know about the real world.

Ward made a huge fortune in 2002 with another long trade in cocoa. Poor harvests and political instability in equatorial West Africa – where most of the world's cocoa beans are grown – led to a sharp price rise.

The 2011 deal was for physical delivery and the beans were warehoused in England and Holland. This was highly unusual, since 98 per cent of cocoa transactions are via derivatives. Chocolate producers like Nestlé and rival trading funds feared that Armajaro's chunk – equivalent to 7 per cent of annual cocoa production in the world – was enough to choke off supply and control prices.

10

The numbers game

Day 3, 8.50am – Vauxhall Tube Station, London

Anisa knew exactly when she had seen so many books – 5 May 2002.

It was during one of her rare visits to the Economics Library at Leeds University. Her final assessment was due in two hours. Anisa hated studying, but student life had been fun. She had £100 fresh from the cash point but her supplier was nowhere to be seen.

That was uncharacteristic of William Blatt. Perhaps he'd been caught? That would be a disaster.

It was a nervous five minutes before William shuffled out of the toilet, sniffing.

'Hay fever,' was all he said. 'It's two hundred this time.'

'Why so much?'

'This is top drawer, Class A stuff. Let me give you a sample.' William snapped open his briefcase. 'Here it is.'

The final assessment for their degree. *Discounted Cash Flows and their Application to Bond Valuation.* Typed, bound, and with Anisa's name already on the cover.

'Two hundred will get you a 2.2. The 2.1 version is a hundred more.'

'How much for a First, Billy?'

'Don't be ridiculous, Anisa. I think the professors might notice if you come top after missing three years of lectures.'

Day 3, 9.00am – The Albert Embankment, Vauxhall, London

Back in her office, Anisa spread her notes over the desk in her cubicle. It seemed that Guy Abercrombie had some investments in bonds, but she didn't know much more than that.

She looked up *yield* on the net and got this definition: a measure of the cash flow that comes from an investment, relative to the market value of the investment. What on earth did that mean? She needed to crack this topic before her 9.30 case review with her boss.

The notes contained three examples, all based on a bond with a five-year maturity which the investor buys for €100. The coupon of €10 is paid at the end of every year. How much was the bond worth? The bit she didn't understand was something called the *yield-to-maturity*, which the notes abbreviated to YTM. The question said the YTM was 8 per cent, which meant absolutely nothing to her.

Yield and time

Then Anisa remembered the single book she'd read during her third year at Leeds: *The Time Value of Money Made Easy*.

All the coupon payments – and the repayment of the principal at the end of Year 5 – were future cash flows that needed to be discounted.

She clicked on Excel and set up this table of times and cash flows. She double-checked that each coupon was worth €10 and the principal to be returned was worth €100.

> **the promise of money in the future does not have the same value as money in your hand now**

The total that came back to the investor would be €150. But only an idiot would pay that because the money would be paid in the future. And the promise of money in the future does not have the same value as money in your hand now. All she had to do was discount each of the flows, using the YTM as the discount rate.

Year	Type of cash flow	A Contract value of cash flow
1	Coupon	€10
2	Coupon	€10
3	Coupon	€10
4	Coupon	€10
5	Coupon	€10
5	Principal	€100
	Total	€150

The discount factor is the opposite of the compounding interest rate

Anisa began by working out the discount factor for Year 1. She divided 1 by 1.08. This calculation was written as $1/(1 + 8\%)$ in the book. The answer was 92.6%.

What, she pondered, was the importance of this? She took out her highlighter pen for the next line. The promise of €10 in one year at a discount of 8 per cent was worth €9.26. She'd cracked the first line.

What about Year 2? This was further out, and made her remember another fact about discounted cash flows. The further away the promise of money, the less value it had to the investor today. So the promise of €10 at the end of Year 2 had to be worth less than the promise of €10 at the end of Year 1.

A light went on in Anisa's brain. The technique was exactly the same as before but the discount rate was bigger ... Of course! The bigger the discount rate, the less the value of money in the future. She took the Year 1 discount rate (92.6%) and discounted that by $1/(1 + 8\%)$. The answer was 85.7%. The promise of €10 in two years at a discount of 8 per cent was worth €8.57.

Years 3, 4 and 5 followed exactly the same pattern. Year 5 looked slightly different, as both the principal and the coupon had to be discounted. But the discount factor for both Year 5 cash flows was exactly the same.

Anisa now had the right discount for the five years of cash flows.

Year	Type of cash flow	B Discount factor
1	Coupon	92.6%
2	Coupon	85.7%
3	Coupon	79.4%
4	Coupon	73.5%
5	Coupon	68.1%
5	Principal	68.1%

The value of a bond is the present value of its discounted cash flows

Now Anisa had to put her two boxes together. Thankfully, it was a fairly easy task. She multiplied Column A, the *contract value* of the *cash flow*, by Column B, the *discount factors* she'd calculated. This gave Anisa Column C, the *present value of the cash flows*.

Year	Type of cash flow	A Contract value of cash flow	B Discount factor	C = A × B Present value of cash flow
1	Coupon	€10	92.6%	€9.26
2	Coupon	€10	85.7%	€8.57
3	Coupon	€10	79.4%	€7.94
4	Coupon	€10	73.5%	€7.35
5	Coupon	€10	68.1%	€6.81
5	Principal	€100	68.1%	€68.07
	Totals	€150		€108.00

She summed up Column C. The total value of the discounted cash flows of the bond was €108, give or take a cent in rounding.

Anisa got another coffee from the vending machine and thought about yesterday's topics. Investors demanded a return for inflation, opportunity cost and the risk of the borrower. The rating agencies tried to assess the risk of a bond. If the risk and the return were married correctly, then you could find a *fair value* for the bond.

Then it hit her. The present value of €150 in cash flows over the next five years was €108, if you used a discount rate of 8 per cent. The YTM was a discount rate. If you thought the bond had a risk of 8 per cent, then €108 was a fair price. So the YTM was the rate that linked up the €150 to the €108.

But what would happen if you didn't think the 8 per cent was correct? What would happen to the price of the bond if the risk was higher? Or if inflation went up and interest rates went down?

An image of a see-saw formed in Anisa's mind.

The interest rate and bond price see-saw

Bond prices go up when the interest rate falls

If interest rates go down, the price of bonds goes up. It's automatic. There's no direct connection with inflation or how the company is performing. It's simply that the future cash flows you're being promised are more valuable because the discount rate is smaller.

It had to follow that the opposite was true. If interest rates went up, then the value of the money promised to you would go down. The discount rate went up, so the price of the bond went down.

This analysis was vital if you planned to buy a bond that was already in issue. Perhaps you thought a bond was cheaply priced midway through its life and might be worth buying. You'd need these calculations to tell you that the return was above your assessment of the risk. Anisa was buzzed-up after two double espressos. She bent open the book, checked her texts and then told herself to concentrate.

Bond prices fall when inflation rises

She used exactly the same bond as before. The difference this time was that the discount rate was going to be much higher. It could be that inflation had suddenly gone up so investors were demanding more compensation for the erosion of their savings. (We will look more closely at inflation in Chapter 20.) Or there might be a sudden spike in the opportunity cost, so the value of the coupon didn't seem sufficient. Or maybe the risk of the company had gone up – and the rating had been cut – because of a strike or the loss of a major customer.

She tried the spreadsheet with a discount rate of 12 per cent. How much would she get for this bond now that conditions had worsened? She knew she would receive less, but just how bad would her loss be?

Year	Type of cash flow	A Contract value of cash flow	B Discount factor	C = A × B Present value of cash flow
1	Coupon	€10	89.3%	€8.93
2	Coupon	€10	79.7%	€7.97
3	Coupon	€10	71.2%	€7.12
4	Coupon	€10	63.6%	€6.36
5	Coupon	€10	56.7%	€5.67
5	Principal	€100	56.7%	€56.74
	Totals	€150		**€92.79**

The higher discount rate (12 per cent as opposed to 8 per cent previously) meant that the cash flows from the bond were discounted more aggressively than before. Now, €150 over the next five years was only worth €92.79.

Bond prices go up when the rating improves

Anisa, feeling the pace a little, steeled herself for the final calculation. This time the discount rate was to fall from 12 per cent all the way to 6 per cent. Inflation and the prevailing interest rate have stayed the same. But the company's rating had increased dramatically because of improvements in its financial position.

Anisa simply changed the discount rate and the computer immediately gave her a new estimate of the value of the bond. Because the discount rate was lower, the present value of the cash flows she calculated in Column C would be higher.

Year	Type of cash flow	A Contract value of cash flow	B Discount factor	C = A × B Present value of cash flow
1	Coupon	€10	94.3%	€9.43
2	Coupon	€10	89.0%	€8.90
3	Coupon	€10	84.0%	€8.40
4	Coupon	€10	79.2%	€7.92
5	Coupon	€10	74.7%	€7.47
5	Principal	€100	74.7%	€74.73
	Totals	€150		**€116.85**

Day 3, 9.30am – The Albert Embankment, Vauxhall, London

The phone rang just as Anisa had one arm in her jacket sleeve.

'Yes,' she said. 'I think I've cracked it.'

'Good,' said her boss. 'I can't see you now. But I've arranged for you to meet with a derivatives expert this morning.'

'When?'

'In half an hour.'

Anisa breathed out hard. She knew nothing about derivatives.

Her boss carried on. 'I've had to work hard for this, so please don't screw things up again. Are you sure you're prepared?'

'Yes.'

Her boss let her answer hang in the air. 'Be at Simonen PanWorld at 10am. Call my contact from reception.'

'Great. What's his name?'

'It's unforgettable.'

'And it's ...?'

'William Blatt. His friends call him Billy.'

A lottery ticket is a contract too

Day 3, 9.45am – Cambridge Station

Welcome to World Lotto!

Are you playing World Lotto yet?

I bought a ticket whilst waiting for the train and studied the rules. They are a mixture of the simple and the fiendishly clever. You have to pick five numbers from a total of fifty. The big difference between a conventional lottery and World Lotto is the delay after the revealing of each number. The first number is selected on Monday, the second on Tuesday ... well, you can work out the rest.

There's another, very interesting, twist. You can sell your ticket at any time during the week.

The prize rules are also different. If you've got one number out of the fifty you get nothing. It's the same if you've got two numbers. But remember World Lotto lets you sell your ticket to another player. Another player could buy your ticket because it's shortened their odds of winning, especially if it's early in the week.

If you get three numbers, you have a gamble. Your first option is to stay in the game and see what happens. You might win nothing, or you might get a fourth number. Your second option is to accept a prize of £50,000 or the equivalent in your local currency. (World Lotto is played around the world, as the name suggests.)

If you score four of the five numbers you get £500,000. No more, and no less. It's a fixed *pay off*. You can, of course, buy a fifth number in the market, but it's going to be very expensive.

If you get five numbers, then things get really interesting. You enter into the World Lotto pool. You'll get a share of the pool, but how much depends on the pool's construction. For example, if there have been many players that week and only one winner, your chunk of the pool is going to be massive. But if there have been relatively few players and many winners, your prize money may be below the £500,000 you would have got with four numbers.

Numbers	Pay off
1	Nothing, but you can sell
2	Nothing, but you can sell
3	Gamble:
	Stay in, and take your chances
	Or £50,000
4	£500,000
5	Entry into World Lotto pool

The World Lotto ticket you hold is a type of derivative. It's a contract between you and the Lottery company, but the pay off from the contract changes as conditions change. If your Lottery ticket goes up in value, you may decide to wait for the end of the game or you could sell it on Wednesday. The choice is yours. On Thursday you may think the price of World Lotto tickets is too low. You might then make an offer for a ticket which already has two or three winning numbers.

The man opposite me on the train was reading a newspaper. The headline screamed *New Bank Scandal Alert!* It seemed yet another trader had lost yet another fortune on deals he didn't understand.

Derivatives get their value from underlying assets

The product which changes the value of a derivative is called the *underlying asset.* A derivative contract derives its value from changes in the value of an underlying asset. It's like a World Lotto ticket. As the value of a winning number changes, the value of the ticket will change as well.

The pay off from a derivative depends on the number of people in the market and the time the ticket has till it expires. A Lottery ticket with five numbers fully completed after the Lottery has closed has no value whatsoever.

Other things that will affect the price of a derivative include the supply and demand (and, therefore, the price) of the underlying asset. But there are always many other factors to consider. Are interest rates going higher or lower? What's the weather forecast for Azerbaijan? What's the current price of steel? Has there been an outbreak of voles that eat wheat? Is this the perfect weather for harvesting cotton?

---

fast facts

Winning numbers are not as random as you might believe

There are certain patterns that you would never think about unless you really delve into how World Lotto works. Like I do.

For example, if your Lottery ticket has three numbers and they're between 1 and 31, it's less valuable than a Lottery ticket that has three numbers between 32 and 50. Why? Because most people choose birthdates and anniversary dates as their lucky numbers, so the Lottery will always be skewed toward dates that exist in a calendar. Since more players chose low numbers, the pool will be shared by more people.

There are also certain numbers that come up because of luck. Many people think 3 is a lucky number, and in China 8 is a revered number because it sounds very much like the Mandarin for luck.

Some people will avoid 13 because of its negative connotations.

Derivatives are the ultimate bad press investment. They're seen as complex, dangerous and the true cause of financial doom and gloom. Warren Buffett calls them 'financial weapons of mass destruction' and, as he's got more money than you and me put together, we have to believe him.

> **ff Derivatives are the ultimate bad press investment JJ**

Bringing home the risky bacon

In the 1980s derivatives forgot their humble beginnings in Japanese rice supply chain logistics and burst into the financial world. Computer trading, the globalisation of firms and specialised quant staff created the potential for vast profits. Investment banks moved away from hedging and began to speculate on derivatives. Instead of avoiding risk, they actively sought it. Soon the markets were awash with the three major types of derivatives – *options*, *swaps* and *futures/forwards*. Derivatives were available over the four most popular underlying assets – *bonds*, *currencies*, *shares* and *commodities*.

Traders searched for something with a price which quickly moved up and down. They had no interest in the underlying asset. The last thing they wanted was a farmer dumping forty tonnes of pig bellies on their trading floor.

---

case study

Leeson to this

Wouldn't it be sensible if all financial books, without exception, told you how Nick Leeson bankrupted Barings Bank?

Here's an abbreviated account of what happened. Confident but not clever boy gets promoted well beyond his abilities. Makes money on derivatives, makes a loss, earns the money back, makes a bigger loss and decides to hide it. No one notices, so he hides more losses. Gets arrested for showing his arse in a Singapore pub. Goes a bit mad and loses millions. Loses more millions and runs away.

Analysis of Leeson's trading 'strategies' is pointless as he was really just a gambler doubling up his bets in the hope of a big win. His final panic trades were the work of a man who had lost touch with financial reality.

It's far more revealing to consider the environment that allowed Leeson to flourish. Barings had very poor controls over traders, abysmal bookkeeping and staff in senior positions who knew nothing about how financial markets worked. Desperate to reclaim the firm's prestige, the directors stumbled and bluffed their way towards disaster. Before he lost the family firm, chairman Peter Baring told the Bank of England that it was not 'terribly difficult' to make 'large, risk-free profits in investments'. A rudimentary knowledge of risk and return – of a level enjoyed by my grad students back in Chapter 3 – would have told the chairman that large, risk-free profits are impossible in any competitive market.

Film fact – *Rogue Trader* is a lightweight bit of fluff staring Ewan McGregor and Anna Friel. It's OK, but don't expect too much truth to get in the way of the story. Based on Leeson's own book of the same name, the film firmly places the blame on other people's trading errors and the unpredictable nature of the futures market.

Day 3, 9.55am – Cambridge Station

There was an email on my iPhone from Karl Honey. It wasn't good news.

Am flying NY this a.m. GA story about to break. BTW, you should have told me you know him. Now I'm sure you have something to hide – LOL!

GA has ripped off several HNWIs. Victims include footballers, bankers, press owners, corrupt ministers and celebs. GYAC, there's no way I can tell you their names.

```
I have great contact in NY who will give me all
the insider info I need.

TTFN

PS GA was on way from Zurich to NY to meet
unknown client(s)
```

And then Anisa rang again.

'We've found a slice of the missing portfolio. Only $12 million, so it's no big deal. It doesn't seem that Guy was up to anything particularly complicated. He just transferred money from his clients to another account in his name.'

'How did he do that?'

'It was very simple. He had the authority and the codes to move the money. In fact, he's left a trail that's easy to follow.'

That didn't sound like Guy. Even an idiot can make money disappear these days, and Guy was no idiot. But I kept my doubts to myself.

'That's great research, Anisa. Can you tell me anything else?'

'I'm one minute away from my next meeting.'

'Please. At least tell me who owned the $12 million.'

'I can't say.'

'Do you know?'

'Yes.'

'So give me a clue. We're in this together.'

'He's a banker.'

'A well-known one?'

'Yes. He's called Jerry Witts.'

12

Out of the money

Day 3, 10.00am – Simonen PanWorld, Blackfriars, London

Difficult choices about options

A Porsche – not the newest one, true, but still a good model – shattered the glass and steel doors of Simonen PanWorld. Anisa stood open-mouthed as the driver walked calmly across the road and tossed the car's keys into the River Thames.

The security guard had seen it all before. 'Happens at least once a year. Normally at bonus time. Some of these jokers get less than seven figures and believe they've *failed*.' He let the word hang in the air as a police car, sirens wailing, struggled through the Cannon Street snarl-up.

'Anisa!' Billy Blatt was waiting for Anisa in reception. He held out a chubby hand. 'Something weird always occurs when you turn up.'

'Yes,' she said. 'That does seem to be the case at the moment. But what on earth has happened?'

'That's nothing. It's just another broker with a breakdown committing career suicide by driving his car up the steps to the bank. It can get quite stressful in options trading, you know. But the money is great, if you don't crack.'

'I guess it's just risk and return in action.' Anisa looked at Billy and laughed. What a difference ten years can make. Gone was

the skinny workaholic economics student who spent a whole
term in the same ripped jeans. Now Billy was poured into a black
power suit whose chalk pinstripes curved with his bulk. A red silk
handkerchief was crumpled into his breast pocket.

'I heard from your boss,' Billy said. 'Have you come to investigate
us? Or just me?'

She realised that Billy Blatt was more nervous about the meeting
than she was. Experience had taught Anisa that people who are
guilty of high-end financial fraud enjoy the process of investigation. It gives them a chance to show off their skills in front of
an audience. But Billy, unbuttoning his peacock waistcoat and
wiping sweat from his brow, didn't look like he was enjoying the
moment very much.

'No. I'm not here to investigate you, Billy.' She watched as he
sighed out his relief. 'I won't even mention your early business
ventures at Leeds to your superiors.'

'Thanks, Anisa. I'll be grateful if we could keep that, er, youthful
indiscretion to ourselves.' He placed two cups on saucers, then
placed the two saucers on paper doilies. 'Then may I ask why
you've come to see me?'

Anisa explained and Billy agreed to demonstrate how options
work.

A trade in the underlying asset is straightforward

'The best way into this is to think of a physical commodity, like
gold. Imagine you've got $1,500 to invest and gold is currently
trading at $1,500 an ounce. Gold – like most commodities – is
always quoted in dollars. You believe that gold is going up in
price. What do you do?'

'Buy an ounce?'

Billy opened his laptop and clicked open the spreadsheet.
'Correct. You invest all your money to buy one ounce of gold.'

The underlying	
Your investment fund	$1,500
Price of one ounce of gold	$1,500
Your exposure in ounces	1

'Your investment in the underlying asset exposes you to changes in the price of gold. If your analysis is correct and gold goes up to $2,100 you make $600.'

Price rises	
You bought one ounce for	$1,500
Price of one ounce of gold now	$2,100
Your gain	**$600**

'But if gold falls to $1,300 you lose $200.'

Price falls	
You bought one ounce for	$1,500
Price of one ounce of gold now	$1,300
Your loss	**−$200**

'Win or lose, you still retain possession of the gold.' Billy tore open a packet of gingernut biscuits.

Call me

A call option increases your gains if you get the trade right

'What's a *call option*?' asked Anisa as she politely refused the packet.

'When you see old film footage of traders in a pit, their heads slicked down with enough gel to constitute a traffic hazard, watch their hands. If they make a beckoning motion they are calling a commodity towards them. So call means *buy*.'

'But how does an *option* actually work?'

'It means that you, the holder of the option, can buy gold from your counterparty at a specified price. This price is sometimes called the *exercise price* but I think *strike price* sounds far more dramatic. And I guess you want to know what a *counterparty* is as well?

Anisa nodded.

'It's the person or organisation that has sold you the option. If you want to sound really pro, you can call them the *writer* of the option. The writer will charge you a *premium* to hold the option, which is another way of saying price.'

Billy poured more tea. 'Let's look at the same movements in the price of gold, but this time you buy the option rather than the underlying gold. The premium to hold a call option of gold is currently $150. Your counterparty offers you a strike price of $1,700. Remember you've got $1,500 to invest so you can buy ten call options over gold. How is it different?'

'Instead of having exposure over one ounce of gold via a trade in the underlying, you suddenly have an interest over ten ounces.'

'Correct.' Billy clicked on another spreadsheet.

The call option	
Your investment fund	$1,500
Premium for one option over gold	$150
Number of options bought	10
Your exposure in ounces	10
Strike price	$1,700

Anisa asked Billy, 'What happens if gold zooms up to $2,100 an ounce?'

'Your option allows you to buy gold from the counterparty for $1,700 an ounce. The market price is $2,100. So you use the option.'

'How?'

'Like this. You pay $1,700 to a counterparty who now has to get you an ounce of gold. He has to go into the market and buy that ounce of gold, which costs him $2,100. You receive something worth $2,100 and you're only paying $1,700, so you make $400 from each option.'

'Cool.'

'Cool, indeed. But what's really interesting is this. You've bought ten options. You make the $400 not once, but ten times. So your top line on this trade is $4,000.'

'I see.'

'What you then have to do is deduct the $1,500 that you paid to buy the premiums. Take that away and you get a profit of $2,500. This is much more than the $600 you made when you bought the underlying even though the change in gold price (up from $1,500 to $2,100) is exactly the same.'

Price rises	
Strike price	$1,700
Price of one ounce of gold now	$2,100
Your gain per contract	$400
Number of contracts	10
Total gains on contracts	$4.000
Less: cost of premiums	−$1,500
Final position	**$2,500**

A call option will take all your money if you get the trade wrong

'Hold on. This financial paradise must come with some sort of downside. What happens to your wealth if the price of gold falls to $1,300?'

'Your options are completely worthless.'

'Why?'

'You've got an option to buy an ounce of gold at $1,700 from your counterparty but you can go into the open market and buy gold for $1,300. You'd be mad to use your options, so you let your options lapse. You walk away from them.'

'Which means...?'

'You now have two fairly major problems. You don't have gold, because you didn't use the options. And the premium of $1,500 has gone forever.'

Price falls	
Strike price	$1,700
Price of one ounce of gold now	$1,300
Your gain per contract	$0
Number of contracts	10
Total gains on contracts	$0
Less: cost of premiums	−$1,500
Final position	**−$1,500**

Options multiply your exposure to the underlying asset

'As the holder of a call option, you've got a big upside but you've also got a substantial downside. Options multiply the impact of risk and return. Get it right, and you make more than a trade in the underlying. Get it wrong, though, and you lose the premiums.'

'What's the most money the writer of a call option can make?'

'They can never make more than your premium.'

'Why not?'

'Writing a call option is not the same as going short on the underlying. They keep your premium but they don't otherwise benefit from the drop in price.'

'So the option writer needs to be careful when setting the strike price. Too low, and they'll lose a fortune. Too high, and no one will buy the option.'

'Correct Anisa. The writer of your call option is in a risky position. Every time the price goes up $1, you as the holder gain $10 because you hold ten contracts. The counterparty will lose the same amount – and now we get to the really cool thing about options. Not only can you make money from them but you can harm your counterparty as well! You now have the right to use the phrase *zero sum game* in your everyday conversations.'

'What does that mean?'

> ** For every dollar you gain, someone else loses the same amount **

'For every dollar you gain, someone else loses the same amount. And for every dollar you lose, someone else will gain the same amount. That's how options work.'

'What else do I need to know?'

'Options normally come in three sizes, all with a defined expiry date. You can buy three-month, six-month or nine-month options. The longer the option, the greater the premium because the holder has more chance of making money. The closer the expiry, the lower its value. Less time equates to less possibility of making a profit on your option. And now, Anisa, you must excuse me for a moment.'

Whilst Billy was in the bathroom, Anisa's attention wandered to his desk. There was a copy of the Cal-Pan report, which had been heavily scored through with yellow highlighter. And there was a photo of a group of graduates, perhaps taken a decade ago. They were arranged formally in three rows but their faces were smiling and their postures were relaxed. In the middle of the group was a face Anisa recognised. Mediterranean-looking, a big smile and a big nose and curly dark-brown hair which was just starting to recede.

'No,' she whispered to herself. 'It can't be.'

13

In the future when all's well

Day 3, 11.15am – Simonen PanWorld, Blackfriars, London

'Have you lost something, Anisa?' Billy Blatt came through the door with two coffees and a plate of chocolate biscuits.

'No. Sorry. Just distracted, that's all.'

'Do you want to know what a future is?'

'Sure.'

'And a forward?'

'Yes.'

'Good. Because they're very similar. I'll soon show you the difference between these two words, but just for the next couple of minutes accept that they mean pretty much the same.'

Tomorrow always comes

Anisa shook her head as Billy proffered more biscuits. 'Who uses futures?' she asked.

'Hedgers and speculators.'

'Who are they?'

'*Hedgers* are people who have an interest in the underlying asset. They're either going to buy it or sell it at some time in the future. *Speculators* don't care about the underlying at all; all they want is a derivative contract that will change value. They're interested in how the value of a piece of paper changes but they've got no need or practical use for the underlying asset.'

'It's a bit like World Lotto, isn't it?'

'Exactly. And the terminology is very similar. The price which is agreed today is a price to buy and sell in the future. That's the *futures price*. The buyer of a contract is *long*. The seller – someone who's sold a future – is *short*. Sometimes the underlying asset may not be a physical commodity at all. It could be a currency or a share. It might even be a *reference item*, such as the level of a stock market index.'

> **Sometimes the underlying asset may not be a physical commodity at all**

'What happens if you buy a future and the value of the commodity goes down?

'You've got a problem. There's no optionality on a future. You can't walk away from it, nor can you let it lapse. It's an agreement to fulfil the contract on a specified date. If the seller of the contract can't deliver, then they've got to go out into the market and buy the asset and give it to the buyer of the contract. If the buyer of the contract doesn't want the asset, they've got to get rid of it.'

'Then how can you guarantee that your counterparty will pay up?'

'Both the buyer and seller have to pay *initial margin*. During each day of the future's life, one party will gain on the contract and one party will lose. To avoid huge losses or gains at the very end of the contract, the contracts tend to be settled on a daily basis. The two parties hand over *variation margin* to each other depending on who's gained or who's lost. Greek?'

'What?'

'Do you want some lunch? There's a very good Greek restaurant called Thales around the corner.'

Anisa looked at her watch. Eleven thirty. 'A bit early for me, Billy.'

'Suit yourself.' Billy opened his desk drawer and pulled out a muffin. 'I guess you want to know the difference between a future and a forward.'

'Yes please.'

Markets and counters

'*Futures* are standardised contracts which trade on an exchange. *Forwards* are tailored deals between two parties.'

'Meaning...?'

'The exchange acts as a middleman between the buyer and seller of a future. Exchange traded contracts are highly standardised. Standardised contracts are much more liquid than tailored deals. A liquid investment is one which can be traded quickly and easily. The market brings a large number of buyers and sellers together. It's easy to discover the price of a future because it's publicly quoted. Futures contracts have easily understood quantities (twenty tonnes of pork bellies), and set dates for delivery of the underlying asset (the last day of each quarter).

66 A liquid investment is one which can be traded quickly and easily 99

'What's a forward?'

'A forward is an *over-the-counter* (OTC) agreement. It's normally one financial institution dealing directly with another. OTC agreements are largely unregulated because the players are highly sophisticated investors. It's very hard to get a price for OTC derivatives because they're private and, therefore, not visible. A forward contract is good for an irregular amount (the local currency equivalent of $107.341 million) of a less popular underlying asset (Ukrainian karbovanets) on a specified date (24 October).'

'Is there another reason why someone would choose a forward rather a future?'

'Yes. It's a very good way to keep things secret.'

Of course, realised Anisa. Of course. She had to get out of this meeting and get on the phone as soon as she possibly could. But she still needed to find out about the third type of derivative.

'What about swaps?'

'What about lunch? I'm getting a bit peckish.'

'One thing more and I'll let you go. What does it mean when someone has *cornered the market*?'

'It's a peculiar term. We apply it to any attempt to manipulate the price of an investment by buying a huge market share. It used to mean that a single merchant had grown big enough to control a marketplace. It could have been beef in Buenos Aires, saffron in Mumbai or whale blubber in Nuuk. The merchant's stalls were so big and so numerous they occupied more than one side of the market. As the closest thing to a monopoly, the merchant had the power to set prices.

'Using futures, a potential cornerer only needs to find the margin rather than the full price of the commodity. This strategy requires much less capital than buying the physical commodity and there's no need to store the goods.'

---

case study

Five attempts to corner the market

Cornering the market is never a risk-free proposition. Attempts to corner a commodity have rarely met with unqualified success. Here are five examples of corners that went spectacularly wrong.

The Hunt Brothers – Nelson Bunker and William Herbert

These two held control over half of the annual silver production. They rubbed their hands with glee as silver rose from $6 an ounce to nearly $49. The brothers had used derivatives to gain their exposure, and had also borrowed heavily to increase their leverage. When the brothers found themselves unable to pay the interest, the market was spooked and silver prices plummeted.

Tin

Malaysia was one of the world's major producers of tin. Why not, thought the Malaysian government, push the price up and make a huge profit? What on earth could go wrong with forcing traders on the London Metal Exchange to buy at an inflated price?

The Exchange quickly noticed the plot and changed its trading rules. New supplies were allowed into the market and the US decided to sell some of its mighty stockpile of tin. The price collapsed.

And the Malaysian government? Not surprisingly, they kept rather quiet about their losses but the damage was estimated at $0.5 billion.

The phony energy crisis

California was blacked-out by the market manipulations of disgraced fraudsters Enron. One trick was to take power plants out of commission for non-existent maintenance at exactly the time demand was peaking. Skill with futures (together with downright fraud) enabled Enron traders to sell power at twenty times the market price. Even the future Republican Governor, Arnold Schwarzenegger, was unable to use his economic genius to save the Sunshine State.

There's a great play based on this fraud, and many of the other ludicrous events that made Enron such a weird company. It's a musical, but don't let that put you off. In a demonstration of high transparency it's called *Enron: The Musical*.

Onions

The Onion Futures Act of 1958 is unlikely to have given you sleepless nights. A number of market manipulations led to massive price swings and protests from farmers. The US government swiftly passed the act to ban onion futures. By the way, I'm not making up this example.

> **▶** *Frozen orange juice futures*
>
> The Philadelphia firm of Duke & Duke habitually made secret payments to receive confidential crop forecasts ahead of the market. The firm's former MD, Louis Winthorpe III, and an inexperienced trader, Billy Ray Valentine, were aware of the scam. They substituted a fake report which forecast a disastrous harvest.
>
> Duke & Duke went long on orange juice, committing all their capital to long futures. When the market realised Duke & Duke's trading strategy, it followed suit and further drove up the price. When the real harvest results were released, the market tumbled and Duke & Duke was bankrupted. Winthorpe and Valentine, who had shorted the future, made a fortune.
>
> I haven't made this example up, either. But the writers of *Trading Places* did.

Day 3 noon – Marylebone, London

I thought back to the email Karl Honey had sent me two hours ago. What in the devil's name had Guy been up to, and why did his schemes all seem to link to me? How had Karl found out so much about Guy's disappearance and who was his shadowy contact in New York? So many questions, and I hated to be without the answers.

Tomorrow's New York course – at APX, ironically – would be good cover for what I had in mind. I had mentioned my planned trip to Anisa but I didn't need her permission for every little move, did I? And why on earth was she interested in gold and shorting? There is nothing more dangerous in the world of finance than a student with a good idea.

The phone rang. It was Anisa. Probably calling to remind me just how close I was to a return journey to a French jail. I had to pick up, but I wasn't going to tell her about New York.

'Meet me in ten minutes in the Accident and Emergency department of St Thomas's Hospital.'

'But Anisa, I'm shattered. And why the secrecy? Can't I just come to your office?

'I've got something that you need to see. Private is better. No one can hear you scream in A&E.'

Perhaps that was a joke. I wasn't sure if Anisa's emotional budget included a sense of humour. I was fed up with her abrupt calls and her orders. This furtive meeting felt like the last straw. I'd answered all her questions and yet she was giving me nothing in return. In a bad mood, I hailed a cab outside my flat and headed across the river. Whatever I'd believed earlier, it was clear who called the shots in our relationship now.

I waited for five minutes before the heavens opened. Ten minutes later a car drew up on the other side of Westminster Bridge. Anisa, a yellow envelope jammed into her raincoat pocket, jumped from the passenger seat.

'Who's this then?' She opened the envelope and folded out three sheets of A4 photocopy paper.

The first picture was me and Guy Abercrombie shaking hands on the Paris train.

'Take a look at the next one.'

I couldn't place the second photo. It was a packed bar, the City or Canary Wharf judging by the suits. Possibly about five years ago, given the hairstyles. Probably payday – or even bonus day – given the general air of drunkenness and merriment. In the middle, me and Guy Abercrombie, obviously both the worse for wear.

'And the last one.'

It was a group photo from the Goodman Rozel graduate course ten years ago. I recognised many of the twenty students. There was Swiss Uli and there was Emily Prentice, and there was Billy Blatt. And next to me, with his right arm around my shoulder, was Guy Abercrombie.

I looked again but I couldn't see the danger. 'So what?' was all I could think to say.

'You told me that you barely remembered Guy Abercrombie. And you also assured me that you hadn't had contact with him for at least a decade, apart from a supposedly chance meeting on a train. The pictures seem to contradict that. Are you lying to me?'

'No.'

I wanted to ask a question but Anisa held out her hand. 'I can circulate these pictures if you want. We have contacts at all the newspapers and financial websites. Your reputation will be destroyed and your career will be over.'

'But the media haven't got hold of the Abercrombie story.'

'Only because we haven't told them. Yet. We're going public on his disappearance in forty-eight hours. If you don't help us, these pictures will be emailed to every newspaper editor on our list.'

I drank two pints of water, swallowed a handful of aspirin and threw my jacket over an armchair. My World Lotto ticket fluttered to the floor. I picked 24 and 10 (Alex's birthday), 44 for the number of my apartment and 50 as a random number. Like most Sagittarians I'm not superstitious, but my last choice was my lucky number – 13.

The sensible part of my brain suggested many good reasons to remain in London. I was involved – however loosely – in the disappearance of someone I had recently met. I should stay, postpone the course and help Anisa with her endless enquiries. I wasn't sure if Anisa was on my side but I owed her for spiriting me away from the gendarmes. She was obviously under a lot of stress from her boss, even though I didn't see why she was so concerned about the photos.

But the other part of my brain, the bit that does the devil's work, cajoled me to take the crooked path. I could go to New York and do the job I love. I hadn't been arrested and Anisa had no powers to keep me in the UK. And seeing Emily Prentice in the third photo had given me a good idea.

It was all about risk and return, wasn't it?

And I could always sleep on the plane.

All's fair in love and finance

14

Currency for the devil

Stop for a second.

Visualise the number four trillion.

It's four followed by twelve zeros. 4,000,000,000,000.

It's too big a number for anyone to fully comprehend. But it's the value of trading in the currency market in dollars. Every day.*

The first time Jerry Witts called me for his pound of flesh was in 1993. He sent a fax to my *pension* in Antigua, Guatemala.

```
We have decided to open up a currency operation
in Latin America. Saiwai sees this as a great way
to attract capital. Please find out what you can
about the market. I have some interesting clients
for you to see.

Never catch a falling knife.

Cheers

Jerry
```

It certainly didn't seem like an obvious move for a Japanese bank. And *interesting* was one of Jerry's synonyms for *risky*.

---

* The real number is $3.98 trillion but what's a few billion now that we're friends? A trillion is written as twelve zeros in this book.

24-hour Forex people

The Foreign Exchange (Forex) market is open 24 hours a day, five days a week. On a single day the same people can trade in Tokyo, Frankfurt, New York and Sydney. London is the most important centre for currency trading because it's in the middle of all these time zones. Over a third of the world's trades go through the UK, with most popular currencies being US dollars, euros, Swiss francs, Japanese yen and sterling.

> **❝ Speculative demand comes from people who see currency as just another risky asset to trade ❞**

Forex is a lightly regulated OTC market. There's no central exchange or clearing house. What you see are computer screens and person-to-person deals made on the phone. Demand for a currency splits into transaction demand and speculative demand. *Transaction demand* comes from companies doing their business abroad, importers and exporters, even you going on your holiday. *Speculative demand* comes from people who see currency as just another risky asset to trade.

The currency banana

Mexico City was the first of many, many long trips for me. I lost count of the flights I took to Bogotá and Lima, the meetings in Guatemala City and Tegucigalpa, the hotel rooms across Latin America.

On one trip I sat next to a young dad in the lounge at Heathrow. He was explaining how foreign exchange rates work to his 7-year-old boy. 'Imagine you have a pound coin and you go to a grocery. The shopkeeper sells you ten bananas for a pound. How much is a single banana?'

'The price of a banana must be 10 pence.' The boy was a spitting image of his father, almost down to the monogrammed initials on their shirts. His dad was JGW III and the son was JGW IV.

Day 1

£1 gets you 10 bananas

The value of a banana is 10 pence

'Very good, Johnny. You go in the next day with another pound. But this time it only buys you five bananas. What's happened?'

'The bananas have got more expensive, dad. They cost 20 pence each now, instead of 10 pence.'

Day 2

£1 gets you 5 bananas

The value of a banana is 20 pence

'Great work, son. The price of the banana has gone up against the pound. So you can say bananas have strengthened against the pound, or switching it the other way round, the pound has weakened against the banana.'

The boy nodded.

'You go the next day and this time you get twenty bananas for a pound. What's happened?

Johnny smiled, confident that he'd cracked the problem. 'Each banana is only worth 5 pence.'

Day 3

£1 gets you 20 bananas

The value of a banana is 5 pence

It's his dad's turn to look happy. 'So ...'

'The banana has weakened against the pound. Or the pound has got stronger against the banana.'

They high-fived.

'Johnny, this is the basis of currency. If your home currency buys you more of the foreign currency, the foreign currency has got weaker. If your home currency buys you less of the foreign currency, the foreign currency has got stronger. All you need to do is replace bananas with euros, or yen, or Guatemalan quetzals.'

I looked at a screen hanging outside the currency exchange bureau next door. If I had £100 and I wanted to change it into dollars, I would get $120.

First customer		
I give	£100	to exchange bureau
I get	$120	from exchange bureau

Someone doing the trade the other way would need to give $130 to get £100.

Second customer		
They give	$130	to exchange bureau
They get	£100	from exchange bureau

Customers at an airport have got no other place to trade, so they're forced to accept the price of the different bureaux that are there. If you're reading this at an airport, look around at the rates at which competing companies buy and sell. Isn't it weird how similar they are?

These exchange places are middlemen with a near monopoly. Every transaction is normally very profitable for them.

The Forex market exists for speculation

A chorus of groans came from a hen party dressed in pink wings. The flight was delayed. I went off to see if I could find a sandwich that cost less than £10. The café blared out *Club Tropicana* by Wham. This holiday hit always reminds me of queuing by the ATM at 4am with Perrine somewhere in Mallorca or the Greek islands. If you're in the *Club Tropicana* mode, you're at the mercy of the foreign exchange markets. Why? Because no one wants to shop around for a good deal on their currency when the party's still going strong.

We took off and I scrolled through the list of in-flight movies. It's fair to say that *Nine and a Half Weeks* is no classic. It's very mid-Eighties, all Versace shoulder pads and matt black furniture. I watched as Kim Basinger gets chatted up by Mickey Rourke, in the days before surgery. She asks what Mickey does for a living and he replies with the immortal line: *I buy and sell money.*

It's speculators like Mickey who drive the currency market. These traders are not planning a billion-dollar blow-out in Las Vegas or buying a medium-sized country in Central America. No. All they want is something risky to trade. The major players in foreign currency are the large banks, not me and you at the airport. They are proprietary trading, using the bank's own account to trade money. Occasionally, of course, they'll do deals for clients.

Corporates which have bought cheese from abroad, or which are illegally exporting weapons, will also have to change currency. A small company will use a bank but a bigger company may have its own treasury, which knows what it's doing.

Investors need foreign currency too. A German asset manager pays for their Mexican shares by changing euros for pesos. All dividends will be paid in pesos and then turned into euros. And when the share is finally sold, the pesos will again need to be exchanged.

One of Jerry Witts' clients had been a farming company called Martin's Platanos. It was based in the Caribbean island of Dominica, which I estimated was 300 miles from my airline window. The country enjoys fertile soil, steady rainfall and a mildly tropical climate. Perfect conditions, you would think, for growing many different types of fruit.

During the 1950s, whilst the country was still part of the British Empire, many farmers concentrated on bananas. In the following decades exports boomed, and soon banana sales represented 70 per cent of Dominica's earnings. But a series of hurricanes – David, Allen, Luis and Lenny – destroyed harvest after harvest. And competitors with cheaper methods took away market share.

A country with a dependence on a single product is extremely vulnerable. Bad weather, or a change in demand for the product, can ruin the entire country. That's why certain companies enter into extensive futures contracts. Jerry tried hard to sell the farming company protection via derivatives. They didn't listen to a single word he told them. A year later they were bust, squeezed into bankruptcy by a rise in the cost of fertiliser and a fall in the price of bananas.

I went to stretch my legs and on the way back little Johnny was asleep. Or maybe he was just faking it to avoid the next round of questions. Johnny's dad had his eyes shut as well, and his copy of *Foreign Exchange Fortnightly* had fallen to the floor. I picked it up, because I was too wired to fall asleep.

A currency deal is a swap of two bank balances

We landed with a bump at Miami and stumbled through customs. In the mid-1990s I often passed through Miami, hooking up with Perrine, who had returned to study modern art. The queue to change money was massive. I decided to slump on a sofa until I could change some cash.

I returned to the magazine. What happens when you exchange currencies? You basically exchange a bank balance in your home currency for a bank balance in a foreign currency. It's nothing more complicated than that. The rate at which you exchange is a price, and like every other price in the world it's determined by supply and demand.

Who, for example, wants to change sterling for dollars? Well, people like me for a start, who are visiting a foreign country and need to buy everyday essentials. It could also be people who are investing in the US from abroad. They need money to buy financial investments or a physical asset like a factory. There'll be firms which are buying exports from the US. These may be visible exports, like grain, or invisible exports, such as tourism.

Some people in the US will need to sell dollars because they want to buy something from abroad. A broker in Atlanta investing in Russian bonds will need to buy roubles. Later, when coupons are paid and the principal is returned, they will need to exchange their roubles for dollars.

case study

All hail George Soros!

To make money from currency trading, you need two things: a smart idea and massive amounts of money. Percentage profits per trade are usually low because there are always many eagle-eyed competitors scouring the markets for deals. If you have a strategy, it will only pay off if you use options or borrow money to increase your exposure.

In 1992 George Soros, Hungarian-born super-investor, was convinced that the British pound was about to take a kicking in the global currency market. He backed his analysis with the equivalent of $10 billion. He was right, and the British government (and people) lost a fortune on Black Wednesday.

Soros – now known as *the man who broke the Bank of England* – made a $1.1 billion profit on the deal. Not bad, for a single day of trading. I suspect he might have bought a few drinks – hell, maybe even a curry – for his colleagues that night.

Five years later Soros forecast huge falls in the Thai baht and the Malaysian ringgit. He was again proved right, and the Malaysian prime minister accused Soros of deliberate attacks on Asian economies.

> Soros appeared unperturbed by the criticism and the occasional eggs that have been thrown at him by protesters. His insouciance leaves us with an interesting question: did Soros cause the Asian crisis, or did he predict an inevitable crash?

Forecasting rate changes is complicated

Changes in currency rates happen extremely quickly. Take the example of a sudden hike in Australian interest rates. Australia will see a sudden influx of *hot money*, speculative capital which flies round the world searching for higher returns. Investors have to buy Australian dollars and sell their home currency. It's logical that the Australian dollar becomes stronger.

Changes in the exchange rate will always have an impact on the country. What happens if the Australian dollar weakens against the Japanese yen? Imports from Australia will become relatively cheaper from the Japanese point of view. However, for the Australians, anything they import will appear to be more expensive.

Some products will be very sensitive to changes in exchange rates. Normally the less sophisticated the product, the more it's affected by changes in currency. Think about buying a million tonnes of grain. If the Australian dollar strengthens, you may go to Argentina to buy your grain. You've got no problem with the quality of the Aussie grain, it's just that the exchange rate has made it more expensive.

However, there are certain goods that you can only get from certain countries. One peculiar example is language. People buy a huge amount of English language training and teaching products in the UK and the US. Students won't suddenly switch to learning Swiss-German just because it's cheaper.

Foreign Exchange Fortnightly had an article explaining why exchange rates change. Maybe Canada's economy was growing quicker than Denmark's. Perhaps Ecuador had to export at any price to survive, or France needed to import loads of raw and semi-finished materials. Who knew whether cross-border deals in Georgia, rich tourists in Hungary and political scandals in Italy would have an impact? There are so many interlinked, constantly changing factors to consider that it is extremely difficult to forecast where rates are heading. I remember Jerry Witts telling me once there were only three people in the world who could predict movements in currencies, and all of them disagree. Mind you, he was drinking quite a lot at that time.

Inflation is always the great destroyer

One thing is clear. High inflation is always negative for a country's currency.

How do we know this? Consider a Maltese investor who cannot decide between buying South Korean won and Lebanese pounds. Some research shows the current situation:

	Currency	Nominal interest rate	Inflation rate	Real rate of return
South Korea	KRW 1,000	6%	3%	3%
Lebanon	LBP 1,200	8%	4%	4%

Focus your attention on the *real rate of return*. I'm sure that none of you need reminding that this is the nominal interest rate minus inflation. For South Korea the real return is 3 per cent and for Lebanon it's 4 per cent.

What happens if inflation drops to 2 per cent in South Korea but goes up to 5 per cent in the Lebanon?

The real rate of return in South Korea goes up to 4 per cent because inflation has fallen. What happens next? Investors who have 'hot money' to invest will rush into South Korea because of the better returns. They will have to buy won, and this increased demand will strengthen the South Korean currency.

But the opposite effect will be seen in the Lebanon. Investors will pull out of the country because the real rate of return has fallen to 3 per cent because of the jump in inflation. They will sell their Lebanese pounds, and so the value of the currency will drop.

	Currency	Nominal interest rate	Inflation rate	Real rate of return
South Korea	KRW 1,000	6%	2%	4%
Lebanon	LBP 1,300	8%	5%	3%

Spread your love

The difference in liquidity shows itself in the spread. The *spread* is the difference between the buying price and selling price of any asset. Normally when you see a price quoted, you can't buy or sell at that price. If you want to buy any investment, you have to pay more than the so-called mid-price. If you want to sell it, you have to accept less than the mid-price.

Service was eventually provided at the bureau de change by a scowling, unshaven clerk. He rocked the classic Miami Vice look of the mid-Nineties: jacket with rolled-up sleeves, Hawaiian shirt unbuttoned to reveal his midriff, and designer shades (despite the fact that he worked indoors).

I handed him the €500 I had left over from France. Scowler's *bid* – the price he would pay to buy from me – was $495. The market rate flashed up on a Reuters screen high up on the wall in front of me. One dollar was equal to one euro. But there was no way he was going to give me $500 for €500.

I gave him €500 and took $495.

The next person in the queue was holding $500. Scowler gave the new customer €495 and smiled broadly.

Why? He'd made two cuts of $5 each, giving him a total spread of $10. And because he only held the euros for a minute, the deal had been pretty much risk-free.

Bid	Mid	Ask/Offer
$495	$500	$505
The trader buys at		$495
The trader sells at		$505
Spread		$10

If you're trading highly liquid currencies – dollars, euros, sterling, yen, Swiss francs – the spread is very, very tight. But, if you need to change Guatemalan quetzals into Icelandic krona, the spread will be wider.

What's the easy way to remember how the words *spread*, *bid* and *offer* are interrelated? Simple.

The customer always gets ripped off.

I was surprised when Jerry left Saiwai to set up his own fund in 1994. And I was shocked when he told me that the fund had paid €75 million for the privilege of owning a Van Gogh.

'But you know nothing about art, Jerry.'

'But we both know someone who does, don't we? Are you still in touch with Perrine? She's got a background in art history. Do you think you could contact her?'

I looked at Perrine, curled up asleep by my side. I couldn't put her through all of this again, could I?

Art for asset's sake

Investing in a picture is very different from the aesthetic pleasure of buying art for art's sake. How does Jerry's artwork, valued at €75 million, differ from €75 million of currency?

The Van Gogh is a tangible asset, something that you can touch and feel. You have to insure and maintain it, and spend a small fortune on security and protection. Any income you might make from ticket sales at a gallery or licensing the image will be completely dwarfed by these costs.

An investor buys a work of art for capital gain. But while they hold the asset they can never be sure if they've gained or lost. The investor only knows the real price of the asset when it's sold. On average, major works of art are sold every seven years. The value of the Van Gogh can be appraised by an expert at any time, but no one knows the real price until it's crystallised by a sale.

One drawback of a Van Gogh is that it can't be divided. You'd be mad to tear the canvas into five strips and think each one was worth €15 million.

Investing in euros is very different. You can get continuous price quotes for your currency twenty-four hours a day from your computer screen. Again your motivation is capital gain, but your time horizon is seconds rather than years. Your assets are *dematerialised*. You'll never see them in real life; they just exist on your computer screen for a matter of seconds.

The markets where these investments are traded are very different.

The Van Gogh only ever has one owner because it's a unique, individual piece of work. ('Owner' here may be an individual, a fund or a specialised art syndicate.)

There may be twenty or twenty-five buyers who'd be interested in holding it, either as a work of art or as an investment or as a mixture of the two. If you are desperate to buy the Van Gogh, you might have to pay as much as €85 million to prise it away from

> the current owner. And if you had to sell the Van Gogh urgently you'd probably have to drop the price to €65 million or even less to encourage buyers to rush in. Whatever happened, it would still take you weeks or maybe even months to receive the cash.
>
> But if you're trading euros, you can buy and sell in seconds because there are many buyers and sellers in the market. If you are desperate to buy more euros, you only have to offer a tiny percentage above the market price and people will sell to you. If you have to sell the euros, you can drop the price a fraction below the market price and the buyers will be queuing up.
>
> Take all these characteristics of the two investments together and something very interesting pops out at the end. The key word here is *liquidity*. The Van Gogh is a very, very illiquid investment and the euros are amazingly liquid.

I never returned to Miami. New York, by contrast, became a frequent destination.

Day 3, 8.00pm EST – Wall Street, New York

I called Emily Prentice as soon as my cab pulled out from JFK. She texted back immediately. She was pitching later at an evening conference to fifty potential clients. They worked for mid-sized firms in mid America. They were, as she charmingly informed me, *schlubs* and *schmucks*.

I cast my mind back to the Zurich to Paris train where my nightmare began.

Conrad had tried to impress Anisa Chabbra with his speech on the value-eroding power of inflation. During the Latin American hyper-inflation disaster, investors dumped local currencies and fled to the US dollar. During times of crisis there's often a flight away from certain currencies to less volatile investments. One person will move to a safe haven currency, such as the Swiss franc, for exactly the same reasons that another will move into gold.

Hyper-inflation led to a massive supply of Argentina reales and Brazilian pesos in the currency markets, which further decreased the value of the currencies. It was simply supply and demand in action, no more complicated than the wheat merchants of Casterbridge I talked about in Chapter 9.

Could it be only three days since Uli shook my hand and said goodbye? I'd gone from Zurich to Paris, Paris to London, and London to New York. I'd not had time to unpack and my suitcase still contained that damned train, which actually seemed to be increasing in weight. I dropped the case with the hotel's concierge even though my credit card didn't work at reception. I needed to call my bank as soon as I had five spare minutes.

I headed off to Greene Street in SoHo for an emergency shop. I checked my iPhone and clicked on a message from Emily.

From: Prentice, Emily, APX Bank

Sent: Today, 08.07pm

Subject: FOREX - Essential Terminology

Hi

Frantic today. Pls can u chk these:

Fixed rate loan - bank will always charge lender the same rate. *6% per annum*

Floating rate loan - lender is charged a reference point (like a base rate) plus an unchanging spread on top of that. Also known as floaters or variable rate agreements. The base rate will go up and down during the life of the loan. *LIBOR plus 4%*

Exchange rate - the price at which two currencies are exchanged. *100 Indian rupees = 15 South African rands*

Spot trade - a deal that's agreed at today's

rate. I want rupees from you and you want rands from me. *Deliver the currencies within two working days*

Forward trade – we agree to exchange our rupees and rands on a specified future date. *We agree the rate of exchange today but deliver in the future*

Emily xxx

PS Looking forward to tonight!

15

Paradigm city

Jerry's second call came in 1994. He'd boldly based his venture in a new part of London called Canary Wharf. It took me ninety minutes to reach the Docklands from Bank because no taxi would take me there.

Torrelaguna Capital was Jerry's new vehicle. He wanted his investment fund to start with currency and art and then to diversify into everything that could make a profit.

'I'm presenting to a crowd of potential investors this evening. Turn up and watch a master in action.'

That evening I went to Stationer's Hall, a medieval guildhall near the remains of London Wall. The houselights flashed off and there was Jerry under the spotlight. No notes, no lectern, just his face projected behind him, twenty times bigger than lifesize.

" Money is the most sensitive nerve in the human body "

'Money is the most sensitive nerve in the human body.' Any lingering murmurs in the crowd vanished. 'Did you know Karl Marx, who spent his whole life writing about money, died a pauper? Don't you think Mrs Marx would have preferred him to stop writing about capital for once and go out and earn some?' The personally invited audience realised how clever they were to get the joke.

Jerry stretched out both his index fingers and pointed to individual members of the entranced audience. He switched to a more serious tone, direct and powerful. 'Do you seriously and honestly want to be rich?' He slapped his hands together and, with the retort ringing around the auditorium, his clients responded with applause.

Money flowed in. Jerry promised steady income, safe investment growth and a shelter for investors' capital. It was my job to find investment opportunities but Torrelaguna Capital was always Jerry's personal fiefdom. In legal form it was a hedge fund, financed by external investors. In reality, it was Jerry's investment playground.

Hedge funds begin with a lie

The first thing you have to know is that most *hedge funds* have nothing to do with hedging.

A hedge fund normally concentrates risk. It may just buy and sell shares in Royal Dutch Shell or trade Greek junk bonds. Hedge fund managers believe they have superior skills and market knowledge to their counterparts at the pension funds.

A hedge fund has the legal structure of a *limited partnership*. Each general partner (who manages the fund) gets a profit share if the funds perform well. Sometimes, if the performance is above a certain target, the general partners get an eye-watering 20 per cent of the gain. The investors are limited partners. Typically between 1 per cent and 2 per cent of their funds is paid each year in management fees to support the cost of day-to-day fund operations.

Early-stage funds can provide spectacular gains. Innovation, talent and an unconventional strategy can all lead to profit-ability. The fund will now find it easier to attract capital from investors, but this may actually be a problem. Fund managers may find it harder to execute their plans because other market participants are watching their moves.

Jerry's fund was a great example. It borrowed money to back more of his hunches. It used derivatives all the time. Shorting was almost as common as going long. Its capital came from a very limited number of investors and it was prepared to try all sorts of new asset classes in the quest for returns. Its interest in art was not for aesthetic reasons.

---

fast facts

Buying a footballer's leg

There are at least two hedge funds which invest in sportsmen. Investors work with clubs, particularly in Latin America, to help develop a player. The funds hold part of the commercial rights to that player.

The upside can be great. Each time a player is sold to another club, a proportion of the transfer fee is paid to the hedge fund. The fund also gets a share of image rights and the income from marketing and sponsorship. You can begin to appreciate why so many talented Brazilians swap the heat of Rio for the driving rain of northern England.

But there are many risks. A bad tackle can end a career in an instant. Talented youngsters may become slothful adolescents. The distractions of success may turn a young man's head. It's a sad fact that 75 per cent of players who play at a professional level at 16 are out of the game by the time they turn 21.

The financial turmoil of 2008 exposed the mistakes of many hedge fund managers. Poor investment choices – especially with complex bonds – turned big gains into massive losses. High levels of borrowing added to their woes, especially when banks refused to lend more money. Some funds collapsed, some withered, some were shut down by managers who saw nothing but hard times ahead. Investors stayed away in droves and hedge fund start-ups ground to a halt.

The scramble to be first

Torrelaguna Capital went into *initial public offerings* (IPOs) big time. Demand for the equity of newly listed companies was

> **❝ The scramble to get a slice of new issues turned into warfare ❞**

massive. The scramble to get a slice of new issues turned into warfare.

Most hedge funds are set up by bankers who have worked in the financial markets. Their links to investment banks are strong. And lucrative. At least 25 per cent of all IPO shares are bought by nimble, well-connected hedge funds. We called every contact in our books and then Jerry made us call them again. The fund bought into forty-seven different IPOs – forty-five of them were profitable.

During an IPO bubble, stock prices rise well above the normal value. Investors in the market try to find a rationale for these high valuations. Soon we would hear phrases like 'Oh, the old rules no longer apply' or 'Get with the new paradigm'. But more of that in the next chapter.

---

fast facts

Prime brokerage

Hedge funds typically use an investment bank to provide *prime brokerage*. Prime brokerage is a catch-all term which describes everything a bank does for a hedge fund. It includes back office work, such as clearing and settlement, for which the bank charges a fee. The bank also provides finance, for which it receives interest. Existing bank clients – especially those with adventurous tastes – can be introduced to the hedge fund as potential investors. (For a large fee, of course.) The bank can also make money by advising on legal and regulatory matters, such as whether it is a crime to push a competitor out of a helicopter.

This area becomes really controversial when the bank effectively allocates floor space to a new hedge fund in its own offices. These hedge fund hotels have been heavily criticised for creating an instant conflict of interest. Although banks disagree, it's unlikely that a tenant hedge fund would look for better deals for its customers when it could just pop upstairs and, whilst asking to borrow a cup of sugar, sell $10 million of bonds rated CCC.

Some hedge funds are effectively stillborn. No matter how good the idea, if the fund can't attract sufficient capital it's a non-starter. Other funds implode because of poor decisions. Bear Stearns (the bank with the most unfortunate initials in the investment world) had to close down two sub-prime mortgage hedge funds which became worthless because of surging defaults. Investors lost $20 billion and took little comfort from BS's apology. In what must be one of the most obvious statements in history, BS regretted that 'this is a difficult development for investors'. By the end of 2009 one in seven American mortgage-holders was either late with their payments or facing foreclosure.

Strangely enough, success may cause funds to close. They become too big to execute trades nimbly. Their transactions become so large that they move markets, pushing up the price of what they want to buy and lowering the price of what they want to sell. Once a fund is large enough to appear on the radar of banks and other funds, it will struggle to trade without its moves being tracked.

Death insurance

Torrelaguna Capital was involved in every bubble. Amongst Jerry's enthusiasms were building society conversions, emerging market convertible bonds, football finance, sovereign debt and many others. Investment banks inflated the bubbles by providing ever more debt and equity finance. They took commissions from a crazed trading market. Prop (proprietary) traders made fortunes just by switching on their computers.

The banks turned off the financing just as quickly. They didn't just create the bubble. They popped it as well. Luckily for us, Jerry always seemed to be ahead of the market. *Leave a little for the next guy,* he used to tell me. Which was his way of saying: *Get rid of it while there's a sucker who still thinks it's a good buy.*

Jerry's fund made significant profits from the normally staid world of general insurance. This is a relatively easy business to understand. Most people are put off because they think it's going to be complex, but that's not the case.

The first thing to realise is that insurance companies are not run for the benefit of the policyholders. Setting *premiums* (the cost of the insurance) high whilst keeping *claims* low creates a float of money. The insurance company invests the money for its shareholders, not its policyholders. So its objectives are very different from those of a pension fund.

A car insurance firm receives premiums from motorists. Its major cost will be claims for death, injury, theft and damage. Claims may be for one-off, small items, like a broken windscreen or smashed headlights. But they can also be huge and long-term. For a car insurer, the worst possible accident involves a victim who is terribly injured but does not die. The costs of medical care and compensation can be huge. (I realise I sound heartless here. I don't mean to. A friend of mine was paralysed and brain-damaged in a car accident. Peter's family received a payout of £4.5 million but it's hardly made them rich.)

The car insurance company takes the premiums, less any claims, and invests with the help of an investment bank. It tends to buy bonds: they are low risk and, importantly, are highly liquid so can be turned into cash for a claimant very quickly. The problem, of course, is that the safer the bond, the lower the return. The car insurance company may also put a small proportion of its money into more illiquid items, such as property and shares.

Life insurance is different. Not all of us have cars, and not all of us have accidents in them. But all of us will die. I trust this isn't news to you.

Life insurance pays out a lump sum when you die. The life insurance company uses actuaries to estimate when their policyholders die. One will die today, one will live to be 125, but the majority of deaths will cluster around 75–86 years. The life insurance company knows that it can take a longer-term approach to its investments. So its investments will be different from those of a general insurer. Forty-year bonds, growth stocks and even venture capital can be added into its investment mix. As the grads taught you many chapters ago, more risk should lead to more return.

The insurance cycle

We avidly followed one car insurance company.

William Anchor specialised in the riskiest drivers around. Typical clients were men between the ages of 17 and 21 who had recently passed their driving test. They had to drive cars with a minimum top speed of 200kph. Living near high crime areas was an advantage.

During a boom, William Anchor can charge high premiums. Its clients earn good money (or their parents are wealthy) and there is no competition. The annual report of William Anchor is released. Other companies see that premium income is very high. They decide to compete against William Anchor.

Suddenly customers have four suppliers when there used to be one. They shop around, and the companies will have to lower their prices. William Anchor, to keep market share, offers discounts to existing customers. Premiums soften and profits start to slide.

Then the recession hits. No one buys sports cars any more. Drivers lose their jobs and can't afford to keep their cars. (Or, much worse, they keep driving but don't pay for insurance.) More cars are stolen and fraudulent claims always increase in times of economic woe. Bonds and shares lose value. More money leaves William Anchor than comes in. The new entrants also lose money. The sector, as a whole, is loss-making. Some of the car insurance companies go bust.

Fast forward two years. The over-supply of insurance has disappeared. The bust is over and there is more disposable income flying around the economy. Young men buy fast cars again. William Anchor, having survived the recession, can harden premiums. It finds itself making profits again. And the cycle begins again.

Jerry had one very simple technique for tracking the insurance cycle. He forced our new graduate hires to phone around insurance companies for quotes. We also checked prices on the newly arrived World Wide Web.

If quotes were going up, Jerry bought more shares. If quotes were falling, he'd sell them. Jerry was skilled, no doubt about it, but his research wasn't complicated or highly mathematical.

And if his research didn't come to a clear conclusion, there were other ways to make money. Perrine was persuaded to return to the fold. Jerry made her head of compliance. She knew nothing about compliance and cared even less.

Jerry stretched back in his massive director's chair, his hands folded behind his neck. 'The directors of a fund called Edinburgh & Empire have approached me. They want to trade oil for their own personal accounts. They've got a team of analysts who cover oil. And they know the buying plans for energy companies all around the world.'

I nodded. 'It's like playing poker and knowing what the other players have in their hands.'

'Or the cards they are just about to be dealt.'

At least Edinburgh & Empire sounded like they would be close to the office. 'Where's their head office, Jerry? London or Scotland?'

'Neither. They're based in Hong Kong. There's a ticket for you in reception.'

That year I shuttled across to Hong Kong four times. Then I didn't go for ... I'm getting slightly ahead of myself. You'll soon learn when I returned to Hong Kong. And why.

Pension funds v hedge funds

Pension funds are based on the concept of diversification. They have a broad holding of different investments to mitigate the company-specific risks we talked about in Chapter 2. Pension funds can only go long, so you won't see them going short on equities they believe are over-valued.

A pension fund can advertise for investors and welcomes all comers. Its fees are based on the amount of money invested, rather than the fund's performance. Some pension funds do borrow money to finance purchases, but (unlike hedge funds) they don't use their own capital for trading. In any other business, setting up a business in direct competition to your clients would be seen as a little bit of a no-no. However, most investment banks now own fund management divisions.

Pension funds make a virtue of their longevity. They will stress their roots in the Victorian age and the long track records of their managers. Hedge funds, in the main, are short-lived ventures.

Day 3 8.30pm EST – APX Bank, New York

From fairly humble beginnings, APX was now a respected player in the markets. It certainly wasn't in the Premier League, but it had enough status to attract 300 delegates to its conference that afternoon.

I stood up to stretch my legs and a huge yawn enveloped my body.

'Conference fatigue, eh?' The man behind me was a sharp dresser with a familiar voice. Black skinny tie, crisp white shirt, a well-cut dark suit and pointed shoes shined to perfection. 'It hits us all.'

'Sure does.' I turned around. Mr Smart was Karl Honey, my drinking companion that I'd last seen in London the previous night. 'What the devil are you doing here?'

'I sometimes write a column for *Foreign Exchange Fortnightly*. That means I get invited to events like this.'

'Never heard of it,' I lied, hoping to end the conversation.

'You've got a copy of our latest edition in your briefcase.'

I was caught out. Weariness, stress and travel had made me sloppy. I smiled. 'You got me.'

'Fancy a G&T? You look like you need a drink.'

'OK.' I guessed there was nothing to lose whilst I waited for Emily's admirers – both professional and personal – to disperse. 'But tell me something first.'

'What?'

'Are you sure you're really a journalist? You're far too well-dressed.'

16

Confessions of a dot-com faker

Silicon ditch

I started to investigate internet stocks as early as 1995. Jerry's fund took stakes in five start-ups, one of which was successful enough for me to buy my flat. Three limped into oblivion. One, however, collapsed quite spectacularly.

SSMF Design was based somewhere in the East London hinterland between Old Street and Hackney. The journey only took ten minutes from my offices in Bank but it was like entering another world, far away from the sleek glossy monoliths of the City. Even the cab driver looked a bit shocked to be dropping off a man in a suit and tie by a bombed-out warehouse.

One of the founders, who seemed to have drunk the world's coffee output that morning, greeted me with a flurry of words. He talked about *B2B*, *clickthru's*, *digital democracy* and *e-enabling*. Then it was *OS, OS2, OSF* and *SFX*, *cool-hunting*, *generation X* and *silicon alley*. He told me *earnings are for historians, mate* and that *cost per subscriber* was the *essential metric* in the *knowledge economy*. And I, like the biggest sucker that ever walked the earth, fell for what was a twenty-minute lecture delivered in a foreign language.

The company collapsed in a blizzard of management incompetency and legal cases. The coffee was replaced by another, more destructive, Latin American product.

What did I learn from this? Technical vocabulary and an avalanche of acronyms are often used to hide meaning rather than to make things clearer. Lots of clever business people have been bamboozled by buzzwords. I was too dazzled to actually ask how the company planned to make money.

Believe me, I paid the price. Mind you, I wasn't the only investor to take a shoeing during the dot-com bubble. The new wave of internet companies saturated Super Bowl 34 with their adverts. A thirty-second slot during the trophy game of the 2000 US gridiron season was theirs for a mere $2 million. The list of advertisers that day now reads like a memorial to the power of hope over reality.

---

case study

Super Bowl 34 – how to burn your money in public

Webvan

This should have made billionaires out of the founders. Online purchase and home delivery of groceries and home supplies was the most obvious and most needed of internet companies. Webvan went from the drawing board to a market cap of $1.2 billion in eighteen months. It crashed because of wafer-thin margins, over-expansion and a fatal lack of custom.

Home delivery was a great idea. But it needed people with experience in retail – you know, companies like Wal-Mart and Tesco and Carrefour – to make it work.

Kibu

This was an online community for teenage girls. Never heard of it? That doesn't surprise me, because it closed down a mere forty-six days after its massive launch party.

Kozmo

Another great idea destroyed by costs. Kozmo delivered everyday essentials to people in cities within an hour. If, for example, you wanted a packet of Rizlas, some chewing gum, a pizza and a Cheech and Chong DVD, Kozmo would deliver free of charge.

And that was the problem. The huge cost of delivering a packet of batteries could not be covered by sales. It was doomed to fail.

Flooz

Now this was a truly terrible idea. A bunch of whizzkid internet experts including, er, Whoopi Goldberg, proposed an online alternative to credit cards. All users had to do was buy Flooz internet points which could be exchanged for goods online. How did customers buy these innovative and rule-shattering Flooz? With their credit card, of course.

Can you see the fatal flaw in the plan? Flooz offered no advantage to customers, whatsoever.

Pets.com

Online delivery of pets. It just sounds wrong, doesn't it?

Burn money

Investors forgot about P/E ratios and dividend yields because few of these new companies made any money. Instead something called the burn rate became fashionable.

The *burn rate* is the amount of money a company has left in its coffers divided by its monthly spend. It's a rough guide to how many months a company can survive before it needs to make a profit or raise another round of equity finance.

$$\text{Burn rate} = \frac{\text{Cash available}}{\text{Monthly spend}}$$

I helped SSMF Design raise £4 million from various private investors, including myself. The directors estimated that the monthly running costs were in the region of £200,000. This gave the company twenty months of funds.

$$\text{Burn rate} = \frac{£4,000,000}{£200,000} = 20 \text{ months}$$

In my heart of hearts I knew that it wouldn't be profitable for at least three years. But I did have plenty of time to organise a second round of funding.

The company expanded far too rapidly. It took on a host of designers and web gurus. People with these skills were thin on the ground and could pretty much name their salary. A marketing blitz involving full-page press adverts and a warehouse party for 3,000 people didn't come cheap. In keeping with the New Lad spirit of the time, the company paid for corporate boxes for the Euro 96 football championship.

The real monthly spend was closer to £500,000 than £200,000. Two months later the cash pile had shrunk to £3 million and I revised the figures.

$$\text{Burn rate} \quad = \quad \frac{£3,000,000}{£500,000} \quad = \quad 6 \text{ months}$$

It was a sign of the times that even with these disastrous figures we were able to attract new investors. It was more important to have market share than to make a profit. We were in a massive boom and no one had the time to be cautious.

The damage done to the English language at this time was immense. Companies would give away products to build *awareness of brand equity* and eventually *monetise their offering.* The idea was to get big fast though your *first mover advantage.* For the first time ever, I heard the phrase *burn money*, which investors threw at companies just in case they got lucky. One of the directors of SSMF Design tried to convince me that *mind share* was more important than cash in the bank. I knew it was all going to come to a sticky end.

Investing hysteria at the time was stoked by programmes on the television, especially in the US, and articles in the media. People were making vast fortunes by getting in early with companies like Amazon. These made the bubble even more buoyant. Investors didn't think about fundamentals and values, they just saw the shares rising and jumped on.

Three boom-time deals that ended in disaster

Caveat emptor – Mattel acquires The Learning Company

In May 1999, just as the dot-com bubble was heating up, Mattel acquired The Learning Company for $3.5 billion. Mattel CEO Jill Barad was predictably bullish about the deal, claiming that The Learning Company was a leading provider of entertainment and educational software. The tough-talking boss forecast internet sales would reach $1 billion in a few years.

She was wrong. What Barad believed was a pearl of the dot-com age was actually a dustbin of tired content. Blinded by the boom, she'd paid way over the odds for a dying business she didn't understand.

The expected huge gains never materialised; instead, The Learning Company lost $1.5 million per day. Pressure from shareholders forced Barad to fall on her sword, with only a measly $50 million severance package to soften the blow. And Mattel gave away Barad's disastrous folly for nothing.

The winner's curse – European 3G licences

Governments organised auctions of 3G cellular telephone networks in the early months of 2000. These auctions were cleverly constructed by experts in game theory: they were run to maximise a government's position as a monopoly supplier of the licences.

The winner of most auctions suffers from *the winner's curse*. Irrationality takes over and people buy on emotion rather than valuation. O2 ended up paying £4 billion in the UK and £5 billion in Germany for a licence to lose money.

The expected revenues never appeared and the phone companies had to write-down their value. A *write-down* is a company admitting that it's paid too much to buy an asset. Total write-downs across Europe for 3G licences equalled £9.7 billion.

> **Beyond belief – the AOL Time Warner merger**
>
> AOL? The fastest-growing internet service provider in the world. Time Warner? A huge media company, owner of big name movies, music and magazines.
>
> In 2000, fee-hungry bankers were asking, *Why not put them together in a merger worth $164 billion?*
>
> Let me tell you why not.
>
> AOL was a dial-up supplier of mind-rotting slowness. Information trickled down to you at the rate of two kilobytes per second, meaning that it was quicker to write a song, learn guitar and go to a recording studio than it was to download it. The collapse of the dot-com boom meant the promised new subscribers concentrated on paying for groceries rather than content. 9/11 stalled the global economy. The two groups of management – one *new paradigm*, the other *old-school* – squabbled as their business collapsed.
>
> The merged entity was forced to write-down the value of the AOL brand. In 2002 AOL Time Warner made a loss of $99 billion for the year and the dot-com boom was well and truly over.

Many of the companies I looked at didn't even have money to pay the fees of investment bankers, but that didn't dampen down the speculation. I noticed that any company which changed its name to begin with an *e* or put a *.com* at the end of it, increased in value. We jokingly called this *prefix e-branding*.

By 1999 things were going wrong. US interest rates rose six times, making the cost of finance more expensive. The millennium switchover (which was a little bit of an anti-climax exacerbated by the computer industry to sell more consultancy) wasn't such a big deal after all. Christmas wasn't the big success the internet retailers had promised.

Journalists started to use the new clichés of the business world: *dot bomb, dot comedy* and *dot con.* My internet friends in East

London rechristened the company as eSSMF.com, but it didn't convince the bank to increase their overdraft limit.

The growth of the internet made it easier for people to buy and sell shares. Firms such as Charles Schwab and E-trade charged as little as $10 to execute a deal. Bulletin boards buzzed with rumours about the next hot investment. What started as a little dabble at work became a serious habit for some people. They left their jobs to trade for a living.

Equities will always rise during a boom, irrespective of the quality of the companies that are traded. Many day traders were fooled into thinking they were expert stock-pickers because many of their early punts paid off. But they never figured a bust could follow the boom. As soon as the dot-coms faded, the stock exchange fell and heavy losses were incurred.

Jerry made a fortune out of the internet. He knew nothing about content or new media or clickthru's or eyeball metrics. But he was an expert on the psychology of bubbles. It seems weird to write it, but we actually parted on good terms. He gave me a generous pay-off for all the extra work I'd done on the dot-coms.

'But remember,' he told me with his eyes burning into mine. 'You still owe me one favour. I'll be in touch.' I didn't hear from him for years.

Day 3, 8.40pm EST – APX Bank, New York

Karl Honey returned with a couple of generous gin and tonics. My phone rang and Anisa's name came up on the screen.

She'd be demanding an update, like I was now her PA or something. I'd travelled to New York on my own account to ask Emily about Guy. In my opinion Anisa had achieved very little in her search to find Guy Abercrombie and his missing millions. Or was it billions?

'You can answer that if you want,' Karl said. Unlike most journalists who've interviewed me for articles, Karl didn't seem to be in too much of a hurry. 'I can tell from your face it's important.'

I forced out a relaxed smile but it felt like a grimace. 'It's nothing,' I said, and I wondered whether Karl Honey could tell I was lying.

17

The brain game

We all like to think that we act rationally but we don't.

When faced with risk some of us stay to fight and some of us turn to run. But we can't choose our response. Some impulses are beyond our control. Human beings are filled with emotions which they simply don't understand. We all have our blind-spots, the biases which others can see straightaway. *Behavioural finance* is a specialised branch of investment which looks at how our emotions influence our decisions.

Perrine spent years oscillating between euphoria and depression. She walked out of her bogus compliance job at Torrelaguna Capital with a big pay-off. Some days she couldn't stop laughing, ecstatic that she had left the markets behind. Myriad opportunities were available to her and, with Jerry's generous cheque, she could do anything she wanted.

But there were many mornings when she couldn't get out of bed. I encouraged her to switch off daytime TV and go back to college. She started a Masters in Psychology, but her enthusiasm waned after the first semester. She wanted to throw her books out. I picked up a slim volume called *Emotional Investment* whilst waiting for Perrine to come back with some delivery boxes.

Emotional Investment was a revelation. The book told me three very important things about people and money.

How do we value our emotions?

Finding $100 will make you happy, and losing $100 will make you sad. Right, no huge revelations so far. But the pain of the loss creates an emotional impact that is twice as great as the joy you get from finding the same amount. Why?

Most of us are more motivated by loss minimisation than by gain maximisation. This fact leads to a strange effect in investment. When faced with certain losses, people actually become risk-takers. They will take ludicrous steps to avoid debts. Nick Leeson, for example, multiplied his initial losses by ridiculous trading strategies designed to hide them.

People feel shame and embarrassment after any error in judgement. Very few of us make a public display of our mistakes, especially in highly competitive arenas such as the trading floor. You can see this when investors refuse to sell a bad investment, especially if it's trading below the value they bought it at. Jerry Witts expressed the wisdom of cutting your losses in typically forthright style; 'You've got to put sick dogs out of their misery.'

Over-confidence is both essential and dangerous

It's a natural tendency for people to be over-confident in their own abilities.

You will rarely hear a man say, 'I'm a really below-average driver.' Women are similarly loath to admit their failings when it comes to emotional intelligence. I bet you you've never come across a woman who's said, 'The thing about me is I'm a very bad judge of character.'

Analysts have to be confident. They always overestimate their abilities in anything they do, otherwise they just won't be successful. All professionals suffer from the same arrogance. It always surprises me when people say they have a hospital appointment to see 'the best doctor in the field'. There are doctors who are rubbish, slept through their training, or are simply having a bad day with their knives. Not everybody can be brilliant. Not every surgeon can be top of the rankings.

❝ All investors feel that they're ahead of the game ❞

Emotional Investment taught me that every trade is a product of over-confidence. All investors feel that they're ahead of the game, even when all the available information has been fully discounted by the market. Every deal needs a buyer and a seller. The transaction only happens if the buyer thinks the asset is cheap and the seller thinks it's expensive. They both can't be right, can they? Someone has to be making a mistake.

Some women are from Mars as well

Emotional Investment also made me aware of another difference between investors.

Maybe it's a masculine trait to gamble. It's certainly a boy thing to publicise any investment success. No man is going to rush into a crowded bar and say, 'Look at me, I've got 4 per cent from investing in safe bonds.' But, if they get a big win on the stock exchange, they're off buying champagne for every woman in town.

My male clients at Saiwai tended to concentrate their risk in a small number of investments. They seemed happier with volatility. Their outlook was shorter so their trading frequency was higher. A lot of men have a short memory when it comes to the mistakes we've made in the past; at a subconscious level we bury them. Women may look at our actions and say we lack commitment.

The women I dealt with were natural diversifiers. They wanted their funds to grow at a steady pace and hated volatility. Their outlook was long term, and they were investing for dependants as well as themselves. Note that dependents for some included ageing parents as well as children.

I may be on thin ice here in terms of gender politics. Certainly there are many exceptions to my rules. I've met 24-year-old men who were petrified to put their cash in a deposit account at a bank. I've met women in their seventies who changed shares like lipsticks. But, on the whole, my theory always held. Mind you, that could just be typical analyst over-confidence run riot.

As Perrine frittered away her pay-off money I became increasingly interested in the interplay between our individual personas and our approach to investment. The head-hunter who got me the interview with the Automaton at APX set up a meeting with the head of sales at a French bank. They wanted to classify investors by their attitude to risk and their need for return.

With the help of a psychologist I drafted a questionnaire. Soon there were other calls from other banks and I found myself running my own business. I was so exhilarated by the new challenge that I hardly noticed Perrine drifting away from me. I always thought she'd be in my life but I didn't hear from her for nearly a decade. Later I'll tell you about the extraordinary events that brought us back in contact.

Yes, I know, no one ever stops reading a book to do the exercises. But why not be the exception?

My investment questionnaire

I think it's time that you had a good hard look at yourself. I'm really happy that we've spent so much time together, and I'm certain that you'll be by my side on the last page. To get the maximum benefit out of the closing sections, get a pen and do the following questionnaire. It'll take about three minutes; any more, and you're probably thinking too much.

Range	Your portfolio
5–10	Income
11–15	Income/conservative growth
16–20	Moderate growth
21–25	High growth
26–30	Speculative

Give yourself six points for answering a question with 'a', five for a 'b' and carry on down to 'f' which gets you a one.

What do the scores tell you?

	a	b	c	d	e	f
1 Age						
How old are you?	18 or less	19 to 23	24 to 32	33 to 44	45 to 55	56 and above
2 Time horizon						
How many years until you retire?	More than 25 years	Between 18 and 24 years	Between 11 and 17 years	Between 6 and 10 years	Less than 5 years	Now
3 Risk tolerance						
Which statement best describes you?	I easily accept higher risk for high return potential	I can accept higher risk for higher return potential	I easily accept moderate risk for some growth potential	I can accept moderate risk for limited growth potential	I only accept low risk investments	I cannot risk any of my principal
4 Return expectations						
Which statement best describes you?	I want my returns to outperform the stock market	I want my returns to match the stock market	I want my returns to outperform investment grade bonds	I want my returns to match investment grade bonds	I want my returns to be stable	I want my returns to be stable and risk free
5 Coping with losses						
Which statement best describes you?	I can afford to lose my principal	I can afford to lose half of my principal	I can tolerate a loss	I can tolerate a small loss	I find it hard to tolerate a loss	I must have a return

5–10: Income portfolio

Your objectives are twofold. First, you want current income because you need to fund your day-to-day living costs. Secondly, you want to preserve your capital. Yours will be the classic low-risk, low-return portfolio: cash, safe bonds, very little in the form of equities.

This portfolio might be ideal for Conrad, the old man on the Zurich to Paris train.

11–15: Income/conservative growth portfolio

Your primary objective is current income, so you fill the portfolio with government bonds and short maturity corporate bonds. You buy a small amount of value stocks for the dividends. You're worried about inflation and so you hope that your bank account pays a good rate of interest.

This portfolio seems perfect for the semi-retired Jerry Witts.

16–20: Moderate growth portfolio

You need a balance of income and growth. You can take some risk, so 40 per cent–50 per cent in equities is acceptable. But you'll choose safe bonds because you need current income, and you might even keep up to 10 per cent of your funds in cash.

This will be right for Perrine.

21–25: High growth portfolio

You want long-term capital growth combined with some income. You'll tolerate some price fluctuations but only for a short time. A mix of 70 per cent equities and 30 per cent bonds will make you happy.

Perfect for Anisa, if she wasn't wasting all her money on clothes.

26–30: Speculative portfolio

Your big objective is capital gain. You can be long-term, so can tolerate big fluctuations in price. You'll be working in a highly-paid area so have no need for current income. You'll choose equities, especially high growth and venture capital stocks. You don't consider bonds or cash for a second.

Guy, obviously.

31 and above: No idea portfolio

You might want to rework some of the easier numerical examples in Part 1.

This questionnaire is online at Learnflow.co.uk.

The right profile

Do you know that feeling when you walk into a client firm and you know exactly how the people are going to be? Certain banks will be filled with Eurotrash aristocrats who drink champagne with their little finger cocked. The asset management firm next door is like a library, the only sounds being the polishing of spectacles and the flipping over of research papers. Some environments are dynamic, some are comatose. Workers may be strung out on too much caffeine and not enough sleep. Or they may be taking a little personal time after a long lunch in the subsidised canteen. Institutions have their own personalities.

In 2003, well after the dust of the dot-com crash had settled, I began a project with a well-known advertising agency. Would I be interested in helping a client of theirs? It was a bank which was having no success in attracting high net worth individuals – people who are well-off but not mega-rich – to buy investment advice.

I worked with a colleague, Yuriko, a chartered psychologist who also holds an MBA from the London Business School. She specialises in investor profiling, the division of behavioural finance that classifies people into types. It works as well with institutions as it does with individuals.

Yuriko's task was to classify potential clients according to their behaviours. She prepared profiles (*typographies* to give them their technical name) using theories of personality that have been employed by psychologists for decades. I told Yuriko that I thought of her as my own version of Clarice Starling, the young FBI agent who studied offender profiling in *The Silence of the Lambs*.

'That makes you my Hannibal Lecter,' Yuriko replied.

I stopped using the analogy after that.

Our initial presentation to the bank's board met with resistance. The director of sales was a blunt 50-year-old called Bill Swarbrick. He came from Bradford in Yorkshire, and what he lacked in intelligence he made up for in self-belief. Bill Swarbrick thought all people on the end of the phone were pretty much the same. If they were rich, the sales people were told to be more respectful and act with deference. If potential clients were only moderately wealthy, Swarbrick encouraged his sales team to use high-pressure tactics to part them from their savings.

'I've got fifteen years of experience in this game,' Swarbrick began.

No, I thought, you've got one year of experience which you have repeated fifteen times. I said nothing, and allowed Swarbrick to believe he was running the meeting. Swarbrick didn't like me, or Yuriko or the people from the advertising agency. He displayed all the classic body language of someone who was frightened of learning. His arms were folded across his chest, his shoulders were hunched up, his breath was constricted in his throat. He laid his heavy gold pen down on the desk with a clatter, as if to say, *I won't be taking any notes because I've got nothing to learn here.*

Classifying investors

I began by telling the board this:

'Every investor is different. This rule applies to individuals as well as institutions. Even if we all wanted the same from our investments – which we don't – we still face different constraints.

'You need to gather as much info as you can about a client in the shortest possible time. It's important to know their time horizon, personal tax position, dependants, cultural background and social aspirations before you can recommend anything.'

I continued. 'Your problem is how to classify a million different clients. Investor typography is the best method we have.' I put up my first slide.

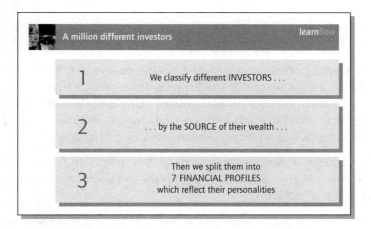

Swarbrick leant back into his chair as if disengaged. His co-directors, though, leaned forward. In that moment I knew that the other directors had a low opinion of Swarbrick. A basic knowledge of body language told me Swarbrick was on his way out.

'Once your sales force can classify, their job becomes easier and their call is more tailored.' At this point, because the rest of the room was fully focused, I felt comfortable enough to continue with my pitch.

	A million different investors		learnflow
1	Manage	We know the best way to manage the client	
2	Sell	We can sell more products to the client	
3	Client happiness	Client feels that calls and advice are tailored	
4	Client retention	We have much greater client retention	

Swarbrick puffed out a thin hiss of air. I believe that learning is about change. Swarbrick was happy to stay exactly where he was. As children, we all want to learn but many lose the habit along the way. Swarbrick was frightened of change, and frightened to have his lack of knowledge made public.

I expected a negative statement at this point, and so wasn't thrown off when Swarbrick interrupted. 'But you've said nothing about the problems.'

'Good point, Bill.' There was no point in antagonising the man. 'If you take a look at the next slide I outline some of the problems with investor profiling.'

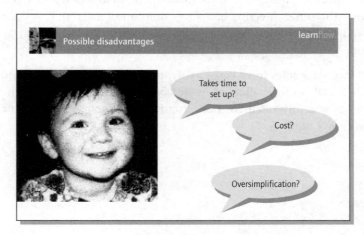

I probably don't need to tell you that the list of disadvantages was shorter than the list of advantages. Or that I presented each disadvantage with less detail and in a slightly smaller font. The word *possible* and the use of the question marks further lessened the impact and likelihood of these problems. The picture of the happy baby raised a smile and made the concerns seem less valid. If questioned, I could justify it as a reminder that we all need to save for the future.

Light came in through the blinds and Swarbrick started to glint. He wore gold cufflinks, a gold tie pin and a gold watch. Gold, the universal status symbol and sign of wealth. Here was a man who needed to display his success in tangible form.

Inheritors are risk averse ...

My first classification of investors was based on how people made their money. Unlike Swarbrick, I knew that an IT manager and a café owner with £500,000 to invest would have very different attitudes to risk. It wasn't the quantity, the *how much* that was important, but the *how*.

My first group comprised people who have inherited money or who have accumulated wealth by working in a big company. These are people who have had long careers with established firms, rather than those who have set up their own business. Senior corporate managers and in-house lawyers earn big salaries without investing their own money in the business.

These people will be risk-averse. The thought of losing their hard-earned capital fills them with dread. They tend to trust their financial advisers once a relationship has been established. They naturally diversify and dislike the unknown.

Also included in this group are the idle rich. The worst subset of the idle rich is the children of the idle rich. They inherit inherited money, and tend to end up friendless and/or in rehab.

... while entrepreneurs love risk

The second group was made up of the self-made rich. They may have run their own business, perhaps even successfully selling it for a hefty lump-sum. I thought of the partners in the advertising agency, marketing experts who have their own name in brass above the door. They were used to risk, and made difficult decisions decisively.

Entrepreneurs tend to concentrate their investments in a few areas and are confident in their abilities. It's important for them to feel in control of their investments. They will do thorough research and bug their financial advisers with their own ideas.

The Cyprus doctors

Can there be a group of professionals more opinionated than doctors? Can there be a population more stubborn than Greek Cypriots? Can there be anything more argumentative than an investment club?

I wasn't looking forward to my meeting in Nicosia. I was helping a fund manager deal with – yes, you've guessed it – a gang of Greek-Cypriot doctors who ran a very profitable investment club. What had started out as a coffee club hobby now had forty-plus members and €7 million in assets.

The doctors had approached the fund manager, Maria Papa-Costa, to run the portfolio on a professional basis. Maria was another one of my Goodman Rozel graduates who was doing well. She explained to me that they were a nightmare client. They were demanding and unrealistic in their aims. They seemed unable to listen to advice, especially when delivered by someone who was both female and younger. They were split into factions and unclear in their plans.

On a daily basis Maria received calls from doctors who wanted to take huge risks, or move into safer investments, or borrow money to grow the fund, or take profits and close the fund. More and more of her time was taken up with their bickering. She was distracted from other clients. What was the solution?

I asked her to find out about each doctor's speciality. She didn't need to call them as most of the information was on the web. She prepared a list of names and job roles for me.

'Maria, the solution is easy.'

'Go on …'

'You just see a gang of doctors. All doctors have had to fund their medical studies, and accept a delay between leaving university and making the big bucks. But after studying, doctors split into two types: general practitioners and surgeons.'

'So …'

'Their characteristics are very different. GPs are likely to be risk averse. They are funded by the state and enjoy many years of steady income. Surgeons are happier to take risks, especially if they have set up their own practice. They are more likely to have an entrepreneurial streak.'

'What should I do?'

'Split the club into two funds. One fund is aimed at low risk/low return investors. The other is at the high risk/high return end.'

Maria followed my advice and both funds ran easily and profitably. Of course, Maria then got loads of grief from both funds for not predicting the collapse of the Greek economy.

Everyone in the room – including Swarbrick – was nodding in recognition. They all knew clients who fitted into one of these two camps. I now thought it was time to leave the slides and tell them of the moment I realised how powerful this technique was.

Financial profiles

I won a big contract from the bank. They asked me to design seven typical profiles for investors to help their sales force. Once the source of a client's wealth had been established, the sales person gauged which profile best fitted them. They also wanted me to write one sentence that the sales person could slip into the call. If they had assessed the client correctly, the right words would create a positive response.

Adventurers

They are confident in their ability and ready to take risk. They believe investment success is their right. If their portfolio performs well, they will claim all the credit. If it does badly, get ready for a vicious, blame-shifting call. A good line here is: *Many investors don't have the nerve for this high risk/return trade-off.*

Hangers-on

These people are moved by investment fashionability. They like to talk a lot about their investments and hate feeling left out. They change their minds frequently and get caught up in bubbles. Often very emotional, they have huge difficulty in getting rid of badly performing choices. They flip their investments frequently. *You don't want to be left behind* will hook them.

Thrill seekers

They don't give a damn about the consequences but love the buzz. Thrill-seekers concentrate all their wealth in a single asset, in the same way that a roulette player chooses a lucky number. They don't look before they leap, so try: *You'll be ahead of the market if you do this.*

Self-confident individualists

They do tons of research, and will look for negatives when others are stressing only the positives. They're hard to sell to, because they are always on the lookout for problems. They will read every line of your research, and take real joy in pointing out your errors. It's often best to pitch them concepts and ideas, rather than trying to sell individual investments. An appeal to their intellectual pride often works wonders: *Have you an opinion on what might happen in the emerging countries over the next decade?*

Technical whizzkids

They love numbers and hard facts. They'll watch screens obsessively in search of patterns. They love technology, so will have the latest phones, computers and personal robots close to hand. *We are forecasting GDP growth of 1.3 per cent in q4* is the sort of phrase to get their juices flowing.

Guardians

They are looking after money for someone else. They hate any type of excitement, and will be loath to change investments. They aim for safety, and will stick to strategies that have been successful in the past. You can only profitably sell to them at the start of the relationship. After that, you will pick up an annual management fee but there will be little movement in the portfolio. They want to hear: *These investments protect your capital against inflation and are very low risk.*

Procrastinating perfectionists

No silver lining is without its cloud. They are afraid of the consequences of their own decisions and lack self-esteem when it comes to choosing the next step. They search for faults in your research as a method to avoid action and are always difficult to deal with. My recommended line is: *Thanks, I won't bother to call you again.*

I stressed to the client that all psychological profiling is broad-brush and reductive. However, the project – now run by Swarbrick's successor – is still running well.

The bank's directors loved my approach. Did I know much about the trickier side of finance? You know, numbers and accounts and stuff like that?

I told them that I did and my training business gained another valuable client.

Day 3, 8.45pm EST – APX Bank, New York

We ended up in the conference bar where Karl Honey sunk his double G&T and then asked for my help.

'I've heard you're the GTM in financial training.'

'The what?'

'The GTM. It's short for the Go To Man.'

'Right,' I said, still a little unsure about Karl Honey's plans.

'I'm writing an article on what happens to the world of business during a slump. I just need five minutes of your time to get me started.'

'I'm meeting an old friend in two minutes. Can I help you a bit later?'

'OK,' he replied.

That wasn't like Karl. Normally he'd be stamping his feet with impatience when there was a story to be told. Yet strangely Mr Inquisitive hadn't even asked who I was meeting.

The lights dimmed for the final session. Simultaneously we turned to watch the speaker.

18

Swaps

Day 3, 8.50pm EST – APX Bank, New York

I always regretted that Emily Prentice hadn't accepted my offer.

When I set up my training company I placed a discreet advert in the *FT* for a junior colleague. I whittled down 485 applications into a shortlist of 50. I spent an hour with each of them, and asked eight back to do presentations. I didn't make any job offers. Some were too cocky, some were too quiet, a few were too academic and many didn't have enough experience. All of them used PowerPoint slides covered in hundreds of words in 6-point font. Not one of them had the guts or the originality to explain a financial concept with nothing more than a flipchart and two marker pens.

Emily Prentice was different. She radiated natural warmth which made you want to listen. She had been one of the graduates on a boot camp I ran at Goodman Rozel, a European investment bank that was perpetually hoping to be swallowed up by a major. Emily left for New York as soon as her training contract was over. She now had a job in the front office of APX, marketing currency swaps to corporate clients on Wall Street.

New York had certainly changed Emily. Her delivery was much faster than before and she abruptly waved down any questioners. She peppered her sentences with *you guys* and even referred to the chap sorting out her projector as *the technical dude*.

Border crossing

Emily began her talk by describing Laropa, a Spanish clothing company. Laropa has shops all over Europe and the Americas. The directors want to expand in South-East Asia. They cleverly realised that women in Singapore (average daily temperature around 32°C) won't buy the winter coats and woolly hats that sell so well in Scandinavia and Canada. So they set up a factory in Thailand and then opened 200 shops in cities such as Kuala Lumpur, Bangkok, Manila and Hanoi.

What choices do the directors have to finance the deal? They could borrow euros in Spain. This will only cost them 3 per cent per annum but the euros will need to be converted to Thai baht. Or they could borrow baht, which will avoid currency risk but which is far more expensive at 6 per cent per annum.

At the same time, Archun, a Thai food exporter, is expanding in Europe. Archun is searching hard for the cheapest source of euros. The company can borrow baht at 4 per cent in Thailand but will pay 7 per cent for euros if it approaches a European bank.

Laropa	
Borrow euros in Spain	3%
Borrow baht in Thailand	6%

Archun	
Borrow euros in Spain	7%
Borrow baht in Thailand	4%

Home advantage

There is a way, though, to have the best of both worlds. Laropa can use its excellent credit profile and long-term relationship with a Spanish bank to get the cheaper loan. Archun can benefit from its similar advantage in Thailand. And then they can both approach a financial intermediary (usually an investment bank) to set up a currency swap.

The two companies swap their loans

Laropa gives its euro loan to Archun. Archun gives the baht funds to Laropa. The swap contract will specify how and when interest payments are made, the length of the agreement and who gets what in the event of a default.

> **❛❛ The motivation of the swap arranger is to be well rewarded for their contacts book and time ❜❜**

Laropa is happy because its borrowing costs in Thailand could be as low as 4 per cent. Archun is delighted because its European costs could fall to 3 per cent.

The exact rates will be determined with the involvement of the intermediary who arranges the swap. The motivation of the swap arranger is to be well rewarded for their contacts book and time.

Day 3, 9.30pm EST – APX Bank, New York

Emily held her audience spellbound and I was proud of my former pupil. A crowd of potential clients had swarmed up to Emily.

'Give me a call, babes,' said a thickset farmer type. 'Your accent is beyond cute.'

Emily waved at me from across the conference hall. She left her crowd of clients and blew me a two-handed kiss. As I smiled back her arms shot out and she started to run towards the bar.

'It's so great to see you!' she cried out as we embraced.

Then she turned to the super-slick journo who had crept up behind me and gave him a massive kiss on the lips. 'And it's great to see that you've already hit it off with Karl.'

We agreed to meet that evening. I was confident that Emily thought I was on a social visit.

Day 3, 10.00pm EST – Tribeca, New York

Offshore pumps and scams

We met at Dive, a drinking den on the corner of Hudson and Franklin. By the time I got down the stairs, Emily already had a drink in front of her. A chunky man was sitting on the stool next to her.

'Has your dad come to pick you up?' It was the thickset farmer from the swaps conference. And, by the look of things, he was settling in for a long night of hassling Emily.

Emily looked at him, smiled, and threw the creamy contents of her cocktail at the front of his chinos. 'Thank you very much for attending the conference,' she said. 'Don't call us, we'll call you.'

'Goodnight,' I said to him. 'You really should be more careful with what you drink. Would you mind awfully cleaning my seat before you go?'

Over the next cocktail Emily filled me in with the gossip. Her social life had been sacrificed for work. Only the sudden recent arrival of Karl two months ago had cheered her up.

'I'm in a massive rut at APX,' she said. 'I thought I'd be happy but I just feel burned out.'

'But you did a great presentation this afternoon.'

'I can do that one in my sleep. Half of them only stayed because they think I'm pretty.'

'I always said you have to use what you've got.'

'I know. But our targets are ridiculous and I'm stressed all the time. It's like management want me to flirt my way to success.' She took a sip of Long Island Iced Tea. 'The spark's gone, and there's nothing to replace it. And then this thing happened with my parents and I realised that I was working in a corrupt industry.'

'What thing?'

'Didn't you hear? My parents lost all their savings to a conman. I can't believe Uli didn't tell you.'

'He didn't mention anything. Tell me what happened.'

'This salesman called every day. He told mum this was their last chance to get lucky and that the clock was ticking. The salesman persuaded mum to take a lump-sum from their house and put it into fast-growth shares.'

'What did they get?'

'Rubbish. A bundle of share certificates from companies that hadn't traded for decades. Bonds from non-existent firms and contracts for lapsed derivatives. Thirty years of teaching at primary schools and all they have left is their state pension. We'll spend more tonight on drinks than they have to live off for a whole week.'

'I'm sorry.'

'Me too. I think this whole financial world is rotten. The police caught some minor associates but the big fish got away. He's free to try it on again. These people are ruthless and completely without morals. And my parents can look forward to a short, poor retirement.'

'What can you do about it?'

'I send my parents whatever I can afford. But I'm still angry. In fact, I'm angry with my parents for being so goddamn gullible.' She slammed down her glass on the black marble bar. 'And I want revenge.'

fast facts

Three ways to scam domestic investors ...

There are millions of scams which can trap the trusting (or super-greedy) domestic investor. But most of them are variations on three common themes. If you – or your parents – spot any of these signs, be wary.

The Ponzi scheme

The scammers place ads or, better still, rely on personal contacts for investors. They promise huge rates of return for very short-term investments. (You know this is impossible, of course, but there are plenty of poor people out there who haven't read this book yet.)

The herd instinct is key to a Ponzi's success. The investors at the top of the pyramid get their capital back, together with a handsome return. The word spreads, and the pyramid widens. The next group of investors get less return, but still enough to stay happy. It's the bottom of the pyramid which really bears the pain. Their money is used to pay a return to the early investors and, of course, to the fraudsters.

The scheme continues until people demand redemptions. Then it's game over and the Ponzi scheme collapses.

Someone once remarked to me that it's a weird coincidence that the first perpetrator of this type of fraud had the same name as the fraud itself. Which just goes to show there's at least one born every minute.

Offshore

That seems such an attractive word, doesn't it?

It summons up images of tax-free paradises, where your hard-earned capital multiplies as you sip one Caipirinha after another. But watch out. Once your money moves from your home jurisdiction it's less protected.

You'll receive a statement every three months which suggests your money is rapidly compounding into a lump-sum which is beyond the reach of your home tax authorities. But it may well be that your money is beyond your reach as well. Countless investors have rung up to release their funds, only to find that the phone was unplugged years ago.

Pump and dump

The impact is as unpleasant as its name.

Boiler rooms are dishonest brokerages set up solely to commit fraud. They bombard clients with a continuous flow of positive stories. They'll be told that they are privy to secret information, must make a decision now and cannot afford to be left behind.

Turnover in the shares, which are normally thinly traded penny stocks, increases. More clients are convinced to buy and a false market is created by the brokerage. When investors are fully committed, the boiler room shuts down and the brokers run off with the money. Investors are left with a portfolio of worthless shares.

... and two great movies about scams

Boiler Room (2000)

A smart young college dropout rebels against his father and joins a fast-growing brokerage. The frat-house atmosphere soon turns sour when the true nature of the business becomes clear. *Boiler Room* contains one great scene when an experienced broker uses every technique to convince a client to buy shares in a non-existent company.

This taut indie movie has very strong echoes of David Mamet's *Glengarry Glen Ross* and openly quotes the first *Wall Street*, but it's more morally complex than you might first think. What's more, it offers the audience one of modern cinema's great rarities – Vin Diesel acting convincingly.

Nine Queens (2000)

A must-see conman caper set in a bustling Buenos Aires. An experienced swindler teaches a naive young man how to hustle.

> But the chance to make a huge score tests their powers of deception to the limit. There's a fantastic ending, where the real villains behind Latin America's most egregious financial con-trick are revealed.

Day 3, 10.30pm EST – Tribeca, New York

Dive was heating up. A steady stream of customers filed in from Nobu across the road. Thankfully, no more of Emily's out-of-town delegates had found this corner yet. My phone blinked with messages from Anisa. But this was my night out and I wasn't going to let Anisa spoil it. She could hassle me all she wanted, but if she didn't know my exact location then I was free to do as I pleased.

'Girl trouble?' Emily asked with an eyebrow raised.

I shook my head. 'No, work trouble. Anyway, it should be me that's asking you about your love-life.'

Three drinks later and Emily was drunk. Not happy, end-of-the-week, happy-to-see-you merry. But bitter, sad drunk. The bar was filling up and I had to shout Emily my question. 'Have you ever heard of an outfit called Cal-Pan?'

'It rings a vague bell. Why do you ask?'

'Tell me exactly what bell it rings and I'll let you in on a little secret.'

Emily's brow furrowed in concentration, as if she was struggling to access a half-remembered memory. 'I've got it.' Her lips parted into a big smile, but there was something forced about her facial contortions. 'I know where I've heard the name Cal-Pan before. Karl asked me about it a couple of days ago.'

'Did he?'

'And he asked me about it again yesterday.'

We sat outside but Emily switched the subject. 'This job bores me to death. I have to deal with hicks like that farmer guy all the time. It was fun for a couple of years but I'll be 33 soon and I want a different kind of life.'

'I understand. But there's more than that, isn't there?'

'My parents got ripped off by the industry that was meant to help them. I'm part of that industry and I feel that I'm implicated. My parents never wanted me to work in finance. I had to convince them that I could do good. I told them I might be involved in financing the cure for cancer or investing the assets of Save the Children. But I never did. I've just made rich people richer at the expense of the poor.'

'That's a bit simplistic, Emily. It's not always good guys against bad guys. Don't you realise what capitalism gives us? It's not just about iPads and branded trainers. Capitalism also gives people sanitation, medicine, water and energy. Companies create jobs and jobs create wealth. It's a virtuous circle.'

She looked at me. 'Rubbish. Companies force us to buy more stuff we don't need. I've got so many shoes I need to rent a lock-up. I have confused what I need with what I want. When that happens, capitalism has won. I can't stand telling people I work in a bank.'

'Why not?'

'Bankers still don't realise how much they're hated. Bonuses haven't been cut. They've actually grown in many cases. All I've done is create more and more debt. For people, for companies and for governments. My sole contribution to society is increasing financial misery.'

Emily ordered two bottles of beer. 'I don't believe that high finance helps people.' She continued. 'Look at everyone who's lost their savings because of dodgy investments. Look at all the families that have lost their homes and jobs because of banking. You would have thought a few bankers would have done the decent thing and jumped out of the 13th floor.

Did they? Did they hell. No, instead they took out their solid gold begging bowls and demanded a handout from the government.'

She swigged on her beer. I saw a tear fall from her left eye. 'And there's this thing with rhodium.'

19

Throwing darts at a random cat

2002 – Goodman Rozel Leaders of the Future Programme

There were twenty of them, top performers who'd been selected to be Goodman Rozel's future leaders. Many of them had travelled from Hong Kong, Wall Street and European capitals for the month-long course in 2002.

The 39th floor at Canary Wharf was bright with autumn sun. These groups are always eager to please their tutors, especially on the first days of their month in London. At the end of the course, stuffed with knowledge and frazzled by a full calendar of evening networking events, they'd be let loose. By then the back row would be throwing paper darts at the hapless representatives of Learning & Development. Somehow, their talks on ethics, diversity and treating your customer fairly didn't have the same grab as how to make a fortune in the financial markets.

Nineteen of the delegates were destined for success. Some of them – Guy Abercrombie being the obvious example – would certainly leave their mark on the financial world. But one of them was different.

Every group has one. The super-smart human calculator with the personality of a small boiled sweet and the social skills of Genghis Khan. Ours was called Robin Bearfield. On the first days of the course, when everyone is trying their best to be super-friendly, Robin didn't make much of an impression. He disappeared in group activities, answered his partner exercises with monosyllables and failed to ask a single question. But Robin possessed strong numerical skills and came in early every day to do extra case studies.

Robin had worked at a retail bank for a couple of years before joining Goodman Rozel. He told me what he did with his salary. 'I saved most of it so I could lend it to my parents who want to buy a holiday caravan.'

I told him I thought he was a very generous son.

'That's true. And I'm only charging them 1 per cent above the base rate.'

He soon began to irritate his classmates. He snapped at a law grad called Sissoun Ward when she left her pen on his desk. He tutted whenever Uli spoke, and corrected Augusto Astudillo's English pronunciation. He treated his classmates – especially those struggling to get their heads round the bombardment of material – with condescension. At the end of the first week, when the cohort hit Covent Garden to alcoholically erase most their learning, Robin stayed behind to improve his advanced Excel skills. At the end of the second week, Robin wasn't even invited for a coffee at break-time.

No long-term course is really complete without its romance. Emily Prentice was destined to break more than one heart in the future, but I doubt she'd ever meet a man more love-struck than Robin Bearfield. He blushed every time Emily came within five metres. Guy Abercrombie certainly noticed and his teasing of Emily was a constant feature of the last week of the course.

'I know you're desperate, Ems, but I'm sure you can do better than Mr Maths.'

'You would have thought so. But I'm not seeing much in the way of competition.'

'Then get your eyesight fixed. It's standing right in front of you.'

Asset allocation and fund management

> ** To understand a business, you have to understand its clients' clients **

After the delegates had mastered bonds, equities and derivatives it was time to teach them how portfolios were constructed. First, however, I had to tell them who ran the portfolios and how they made money. To understand a business, you have to understand its clients' clients. So, to understand how an investment bank made money from fund managers, I had to show them why people entrust their money to a fund management company.

Fund management clients are institutions and individuals

Fund managers (FMs) deal with two groups of client. The first group comprises insurance companies, pension funds, charities and large firms. These are *institutional investors* who have large amounts of money to invest.

The second group is *private investors*. These include *high net worth* (HNW) individuals who invest directly in funds. You'll hear phrases like *wealth management* and *portfolio private banking* with regard to HNWs. The exact name seems to depend on the classiness of the office and the relative poshness of the salesperson. A big part of this second group will also be smaller domestic investors who invest via a *collective investment scheme* (CIS) which pools together their money into a single big fund.

Fund management firms earn fees from their clients. The fee is primarily based on the amount of money invested (*We charge you 1 per cent of the year-end valuation of your fund*) but there may be additional fees for superior performance. The performance of funds – and the managers who run them – is best assessed over periods of at least five years. This should iron out lucky and unlucky years. So FMs shouldn't suffer from the short-terminism that pressurises traders.

Investment management fees will detract from an investor's return

Remember our earlier work on the *time value of money* (see Chapter 6) Imagine that twenty-five years ago you lived in an inflation-free paradise. You were gifted £100,000. An investment company promised you 11 per cent return per annum. In a world without fees, the power of compounding would grow your £100,000 to £1,358,546.

Opening investment	£100,000
Years	25
Average return	11%
Opening charge	0%
Annual fee	0%
Closing value	£1,358,546

But investors are charged for either entering or leaving the fund. They also pay an annual fee, dependent on the level of service they get and the amount of money they have invested.

Let's say your neighbour had exactly the same gift, timeframe and returns as you. But she paid an opening charge of 4 per cent and an annual fee of 3 per cent. Her total – £657,454 – was less than half of what you received.

Opening investment	£100,000
Years	25
Average return	11%
Opening charge	4%
Annual fee	3%
Closing value	£657,454

You can really see how opening charges and annual fees destroy the power of compounding with this example. Your neighbour's investment pool was immediately reduced to £96,000 because of the 4 per cent opening charge. And her annual return is really 8 per cent, because she has lost 3 per cent in annual fees.

Get active

Share analysts make a living by convincing clients that the market is wrong. They believe that their superior insight can identify investments which are mispriced. If you think back to Chapter 3, the analyst decides that the As are clear buys and the Bs should be dropped.

Active managers believe in stock-picking. Rather than choosing to invest a basket of equities – like the NASDAQ 500 or the EUROTOP 300 – they plump for a single company in a sector. An analyst's recommendation implies that the market is wrong in pricing the risk and return of a stock. If the analyst is believed, they will receive commission from the fund when it buys or sells investments. Financial research exists to create income for the investment bank. You don't see many lengthy reports with a *hold* recommendation. No analyst will waste time publishing research that doesn't generate commission income.

Half of the actively-managed funds will outperform the index. However, the other side of this inescapable truth remains. Half of the actively-managed funds must underperform the index. Fund managers make bad decisions and may be blinded by their past successes. They may be foolish or unlucky but no more than 50 per cent of fund managers can outperform the index.

Once the extra costs of active management are deducted from the investor's return, the net returns flowing to investors are even lower. Fund managers are well paid because of their experience, knowledge of sectors and expertise in picking stocks. Analysts, researchers, administrators and traders are all well paid. Bloomberg and Reuters screens – which supply news and financial information – are expensive. Trading creates transaction costs and taxes, which all detract from the investor's income. The FM needs marketing and sales staff to bring in the money and an extensive back office to track transactions and calculate valuations.

My personal view supports the existence of analysts but only in new sectors or markets which are not saturated by coverage. Once you have forty or fifty analysts covering the same stock, there is very little scope for one person to uncover any new information.

---

fast facts

Assuming a passive position

Imagine that everything you've been told about investment analysis was wrong. What would you do if you believed that trading shares was a waste of time and money? You would probably choose a passive investment fund.

Passive managers believe that share prices – especially of the large cap stocks which dominate an index – are right. All information that can be known about the company, its customers, its bosses, its products and even its future growth is already contained in the share price. If the market is correct in pricing shares, then there is nothing to be gained from switching from one stock to another.

They create portfolios which replicate the main index of a country. These are often known as *tracker funds* because they closely track the index. No attempt is made to outperform the market, so passive management fees should be tiny in comparison with their active competitors.

Buying a passive fund is not without its nervous moments. You have to stick with your portfolio, even if you think the market is about to plummet. If you sell, you have become active.

Money fact – Approximately 40 per cent of money currently invested in the world's equity markets is in passive funds. The higher this percentage rises, the less attractive a career as an analyst will appear.

On Margate sands

Portfolios are all about diversification

My parents moved from London to Margate* when I was nine months old. I had no say in the matter but I have regretted their decision ever since.

During the summer holiday I worked in an ice-cream hut on Margate beach and I also collected tickets in the cinema attached to the iconic fairground, Dreamland.

Both businesses start the summer worth exactly £100,000. The major factor changing their valuation is the weather. As the sun grows hotter, tourists eat more ice creams and avoid the cinema. But if it starts to rain, the sunbathers buy less ice cream and head into the cinema. Each business owns assets which have a market value of £100,000.

Let's look at things from the perspective of the cinema owner. The average summer temperature in Margate is 25°C. If the weather gets hotter than this, no one goes to the cinema because they're all cooling off on the beach. But if the weather goes bad – which is not exactly unknown for the British summer – people will buy tickets (and drinks and popcorn, where the cinema really makes its profits). So, for each degree of extra cold the value of the cinema rises by £25,000.

Cinema

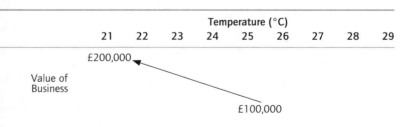

	Temperature (°C)								
	21	22	23	24	25	26	27	28	29

£200,000

Value of
Business

£100,000

---

* If you're not from the UK, I want you to think of Margate as a sophisticated seaside paradise, patronised by rock stars, celebrities, artists and the mega wealthy. If you are from the UK, just keep quiet.

Flip this around and consider the ice-cream hut. Each degree the thermometer rises above 25°C is good news. There will be bigger queues and more sales. The value of the business goes up by £25,000.

Ice cream hut

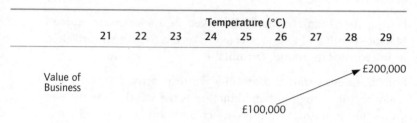

				Temperature (°C)				
21	22	23	24	25	26	27	28	29

Value of Business

£200,000

£100,000

What happens if we invest £50,000 to buy half of each of the two businesses? We now have a portfolio worth £100,000 (£50.000 each in the two businesses).

Weather risk is cancelled out by holding the balanced pair. We only make £12,500 for each degree of change because we only hold half our previous investment. But we make it regardless of whether the temperature has gone up or down.

Shared portfolio

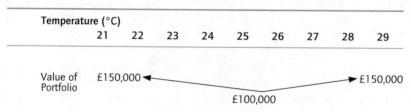

Temperature (°C)								
21	22	23	24	25	26	27	28	29

Value of Portfolio £150,000

£100,000

£150,000

By diversifying on Margate Sands, we got rid of weather risk. If more people visit the town, then the value of our portfolio of assets will rise. Our big risk – which we cannot diversify away – is if the town becomes unpopular and no one turns up.

Different assets perform differently according to economic circumstances.

---

fast facts

The ups and downs of correlation

In the financial world, *correlation* is a measure of how two investments move in relation to each other. Correlation can be as high as PLUS 1 or as low as MINUS 1.

Two cod-fishing firms based in the same harbour will be closely correlated – they face very similar patterns of cost and demand. Their correlation will be close to PLUS 1.

Coffee beans and coffee shops are negatively correlated – if the price of coffee goes up, shares in Starbucks go down because the company's raw materials are more expensive. Their correlation will be close to MINUS 1.

Some assets are not correlated at all – the price of wood pulp should move independently of Israeli government bonds. Their correlation will be 0.

Diversification – through assets, countries, sectors and individual companies – automatically improves the relationship between risk and return. When one asset zigs, another one zags. If the price of oil goes up, you'll make loads of money if you're long oil via a future or the underlying commodity. But shares of companies which use a lot of oil – airlines being the clearest example – will fall. Over time the ups and downs cancel each other out and you're left with a smoothed upward line.

fast facts

How diversification works

I got a call from an estate agent who was marketing a new development of one-bedroom flats on Chelsea Bridge. There would be 100 identical flats and each one would cost £750,000. The agent informed me that this was the going rate for a bijou pied-à-terre in an urban environment. I took a look. They were rabbit hutches between a railway line and a scrapyard but people will buy anything in London.

While I was there a developer friend called me. Property Pavlou asked me if I would like to join his syndicate. He planned to buy all 100 flats for £75,000,000. I could buy a 1 per cent stake in the syndicate for £750,000.

What are the differences between buying one flat and buying 1 per cent of a hundred flats via a syndicate?

I've got control over my single flat. It's mine to sell or rent. All the rewards of ownership flow to me. And it may be that my flat goes up in value more than the other ninety-nine. Perhaps my wonderful taste in interior design sparks a bidding war. Or my view is suddenly improved by a new park where the scrapyard used to be. If I make the right choice, my flat outperforms the market.

But I also carry all of the risks. If there's a void period I will still need to pay the mortgage. If pipes burst and flood the flat I'll have to find money for the repairs. Perhaps the scrapyard expands into asbestos disposal. If events turn against me, my flat underperforms the market.

The syndicate averages my return. If three flats are empty, ninety-seven will be producing income. Repairs in one flat will be paid by cash flow from the others. Some flats will outperform, some will underperform. My overall return will reflect the average return on the whole block of flats. However, I will have to hand over some of my return to Property Pavlou for organising the investors and managing the property.

> The syndicate offers diversification which spreads my risk. I give up the chance of an outperforming flat and avoid the risk of an underperforming one. I avoid specific risk. The one risk I can't diversify away is if the whole building collapses. I can only avoid that by shunning the entire world of property investment.

Asset allocation decides broad investment categories

An investor has unlimited choices. They could keep their money in cash, buy bonds or equities, or could venture into investment property and commodities. Perhaps art and precious metals would appeal, or maybe currency, derivatives or even celebrity memorabilia.

Let's assume that the investor is limited to just three of these asset classes – cash, bonds and equities. Cash is very low risk. The return is affected by changes in the interest rate, and inflation will take a chunk. Bonds are relatively safe, depending on their rating. Inflation, interest rates and risk will change the return on a bond. Equities, as I'm sure you now know, are the riskiest class.

❝ **The most important decision made by a fund management company is asset allocation** ❞

The most important decision made by a fund management company is *asset allocation*. We need cash for liquidity and rainy days. The bonds give us income and should preserve capital. And we have equities which, depending on our selection, give us both dividend income and capital growth.

What, then, is the ideal proportion of cash, bonds and equities? There is no simple answer to that, no one-size-fits-all approach that will suit everyone. As Chapter 17 showed us, we are all individuals when it comes to investing.

Day 3, 11.30pm EST – Tribeca, New York

Dive was packed now. We were surrounded by men who looked like models and women sporting Mulberry croc shoulder bags.

Each time the door opened people stared in case a film star or rock god was coming in to party. I, however, had rather more pressing things on my mind.

'What's rhodium?' I wondered if Emily could hear the panic in my voice.

'It's the world's rarest chemical. And the most expensive.'

'More expensive than gold?'

'Yes.'

'Why? I've never heard of it.'

'Only twenty-five tonnes of rhodium is produced each year. And demand far exceeds supply. It trades at about one hundred times the price of silver.'

'What's so special about rhodium?'

'It has a higher melting point than platinum. It resists corrosion. A tiny fleck of rhodium is enough to stop silver from tarnishing. It's essential for catalytic converters in cars because it makes exhaust fumes less toxic. Because there's no substitute, the whole automobile industry relies on it.'

'Where does rhodium come from?'

'It's mined in South Africa, Ontario and in the Ural mountains. The problem has been that no natural source of pure rhodium has ever been discovered. It's always found mixed in with other metals – gold, platinum, palladium. A new source has just come online.'

'Where?'

'*Where* is not the right question. You should be asking *what*.'

'OK.' I tried hard to contain my eagerness. 'What's the source of the rhodium?'

'Spent nuclear fuel.'

'But who on earth would buy a chemical extracted from nuclear fuel rods? The risks must be enormous.'

'Yes. But a wise man once told me that where there's risk, there's return. And lots of risk often equates to very significant return.'

'Are you serious? Is there even a market for rhodium?'

'There's a fairly simple spot market, but prices are only quoted twice a day. All trades are over-the-counter. The price is incredibly volatile. For instance, when the US car industry collapsed in 2008, the price fell off a cliff. It's a market ready to be plucked. Look what happened with tantalum.'

Tantalum. Another strange name from my Cal-Pan list.

'It comes from columbite-tantalite: coltan for short.' Emily had certainly done her research. 'Coltan is only found in soils which are at least three billion years old. It makes tantalum capacitors, which are essential for mobile phones. Think about this for a second. There are four billion mobiles in the world, and each one needs a tiny sliver of tantalum. There is no alternative, no man-made substitute. APX plan to launch options over rhodium in the next three months. And I plan to stop them.'

'But selling rhodium isn't illegal.'

'True. And much of the world's supply does come from legitimate mines. But a black market appeared a few years back in the Congo, in an area close to the borders with Rwanda and Uganda. An illegal mine, on land stolen from farmers, run with slave labour. Ten thousand innocent civilians murdered, many more driven from their homelands. Children as young as seven and eight forced to pan for materials with a gun held to their heads.'

Eight years old. Younger than my nephew Alex.

'There's no regulation and no control. Rhodium ore passes from the miners to the processors to traders in other countries. There's no trail. You can smuggle out a kilo of rhodium in your hand luggage and sell it for 200,000 bucks. There are even people pushing rhodium on eBay, with no questions asked.'

She slammed down the bottle on the bar. 'I don't want heads of state to be assassinated so a corrupt mining company can prosper.

I don't want governments bribed, the environment destroyed, human rights violated. These people have women raped in front of their families. They've displaced millions of refugees and have deliberately spread AIDS to destroy tribes. We all want laptops and games consoles but we don't want to accept that people are dying every day to fulfil our needs. There's a direct link between that phone in your hand and the devastation in Africa.'

We stumbled outside. The sudden shock of a cold night in New York made us shiver. Emily lit a cigarette, the smoke curling up towards my face. 'It's *Heart of Darkness* for the twenty-first century. If we can find trillions of dollars to save investment banks and hedge funds, why can't we find billions to end hunger and disease? We could cover the Sahara desert with solar panels and the energy crisis will be solved immediately. I've seen the research and the project has been hidden because the oil producers and the energy companies can't make a profit out of it.'

Emily lit another cigarette from the butt of her last one. 'A few people have got extremely wealthy. I bet you all of them were very rich before. I've seen what hedge funds do. They take money from greedy people and give it to even greedier people. I don't want to be part of any system that does that.'

'Then why don't you leave?'

'I'm just about to. But first I'm going to destroy APX. Or at least a tiny part of it.'

Laying all the economists end to end

The bottom line

Day 4, 8.00am EST – New York

The next morning my credit card was again declined at the hotel. Luckily Emily was on hand to sort out the bill and walk with me the short distance to the bank. The APX delegates are sharp and there were a lot of them. I, however, am hung-over and on my own. These are not ideal conditions for teaching. Some instructors joke that they can do their courses in their sleep. Sadly, that's not an option when you've got 120 of New York's finest in front of you.

I was at APX for a day to teach the group about economics. I started by hanging up a huge banner made of three pieces of flipchart taped together. This is a good technique because it immediately tells the delegates that the course is going to be interactive, not just a procession of slides.

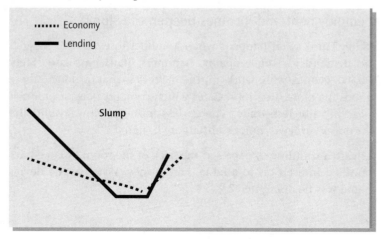

Busts and burnt fingers

'Look at these two lines. The dotted line represents how the economy is doing. It tells us if the economy is growing or shrinking, and how quickly. The solid black line shows the value of all the mortgages in a country. What can you see when we are in a slump?'

One great aspect of big groups – especially in the US – is that there's always someone who wants to make an early impression. A sleek-looking guy in a buttoned-up suit was quick to answer. 'The level of mortgages is very low. It's like the bank doesn't want to lend to anyone.'

'Correct. Banks resist lending because their fingers have been burnt in the recent past. Anybody looking to move house – or a first-time home buyer looking for a leg up on to the property ladder – finds it extremely difficult to get a mortgage. There's a considerable knock-on effect from this slump in lending. If you work for companies which sell houses, cars or holidays you are at risk. Decreased demand for your products and services means work will dry up. If your company closes, your suppliers will suffer.'

'I don't get it,' said a young woman in thick-rimmed black glasses. 'Can you be more small picture?'

Lower employment and incomes deepen the slump

'Sure. Think what happens when a builder loses his job. There's no demand for bricks, paint, hammers, hard hats and safety boots. People who work in the factories that produce these goods may lose their jobs. Cafés which cook breakfast and lunch near the site lose trade. There's less money flying around the economy, so fewer non-essentials are bought.'

I heard a shuffling of papers at the back of the room. A latecomer bundled himself on to a table. Karl Honey. What in the devil's name was he doing here?

The stumble from recession to depression

The sleek-looking guy asked a second question. 'What happens to a government during a slump?'

'Unemployment rates rise, so a government has to spend more on benefits. And, in a classic double-whammy, they receive less money from income tax because fewer people are working. The take from corporation tax also falls because companies find it harder to make a profit. Some even go bust. Everybody in the economy – individuals, companies and government – becomes profoundly pessimistic.'

Another woman, pencil thin and with a Russian accent, put up her hand. 'Is there a formal definition of a recession?'

'One definition of a *recession* is two successive quarters of falling GDP (GDP, roughly speaking, is our dotted line). If you see the general trend is down for six months or more, you know that a country is in a slump.'

'What's the difference between a recession and a depression?' she asked.

❝ A depression follows a big drop in GDP and is prolonged ❞

'A *depression* follows a big drop in GDP and is prolonged. It can have a terrible psychological impact on individuals and the nation as a whole. General expectations about employment and wealth will drop and people will start to save money rather than invest in the economy. This tendency actually reinforces the cycle.'

I pointed to the bottom edge of the mega-graph.

'If these two lines – changes in the economy and lending – continue to bump along the bottom the depression will last. Banks don't want to lend, consumers don't want to spend, businesses don't want to hire any more people, and the government doesn't want to build any new infrastructure projects. Unemployment then rears its ugly head.'

The terrible cost of unemployment

---

fast facts

Unemployment

Our ancestors lived off the land. Nearly everybody knew how to build shelters, grow crops or hunt wild animals. The Industrial Revolution changed all this. It marked the birth of the middleman and the end of the hunters and gatherers. The weekly wage was invented, and people become dependent on the money which bought food rather than the food itself. This marks the beginning of modern employment. And with employment, of course, came unemployment.

The formal definition of an unemployed person is someone who wants work – and is actively looking for work – but hasn't been employed for past four weeks. A simple formula calculates the unemployment rate:

$$\text{Unemployment rate} = \frac{\text{Unemployed workers}}{\text{Total available workforce}}$$

Consider a country where the total available workforce is 10,000,000. If 700,000 of the workforce is unemployed, the unemployment rate is 7 per cent. Be clear that we exclude all people who are *not* looking for work from the calculation. We don't count students, homemakers, prisoners or the idle rich.

$$\text{Unemployment rate} = \frac{700,000}{10,000,000} = 7\%$$

But, as with so many things in economics, complexity appears as soon as we try to simplify. How, for example, do we deal with unemployed people who don't claim benefits? Or students who have multiple part-time jobs? There's always a certain amount of unemployment which is hidden. People who are on retraining schemes or gap years won't be included in these statistics.

Cyclical unemployment rises during a recession

'Cyclical unemployment occurs when total demand in the economy for goods and services isn't sufficient to create full employment. A vicious cycle is set in motion: less money in the economy means less demand for goods and services, which leads to higher unemployment and even less money in the economy. Cyclical unemployment is terrible because it is both involuntary and long-term.

'A high level of cyclical unemployment creates numerous financial and social problems. It's difficult for the unemployed to meet their financial obligations. Mortgages and rents won't be paid, so banks and landlords suffer from bad debts.

'And there's a huge emotional cost to be borne. People who are long-term unemployed and are desperately looking for work tend to suffer from mental stress and low self-esteem. A sense of futility may engulf the country, and this combination of long-term unemployment and financial stress may make people take unsuitable work. Having a job that doesn't use your skills and is badly paid is a further cause of psychological problems. It's been estimated that being unemployed for significant periods of your working life will reduce your life expectancy by an average of seven years.'

Coming out of recession

Cuts in the interest rate stimulate demand

I was back in my stride now, helped on by a couple of coffees and two litres of mineral water. I looked at the back row and Karl Honey was still staring at me. The earliest I could find out what he was up to would be break-time. Before that, I had to explain to my group how a government slashes interest rates to end the slump.

'If interest rates go down, investors have less incentive to save. Because the return on cash is very low, they may think it's worthwhile to go into equities. It may also encourage them to borrow money, either to invest in financial assets or to buy property.

'Companies will also benefit because their financing is cheaper. Projects that would previously have been rejected now appear attractive. If they go ahead, there'll be more employment and more purchases of goods and services. The economy will begin to grow.

'One extreme version of this policy was seen during the last crisis in Sweden. The Swedish government fixed interest rates at minus 0.25 per cent. Why on earth would they do something which – at first sight – seems illogical?'

'To discourage banks from holding on to their deposits,' answered the Russian woman. 'The bank is penalised for playing safe.'

'Exactly. The more conservative the bank, the more it will keep deposits with the central bank rather than granting loans. The Swedish government wanted the banks to create an environment of easy credit so the economy could grow.

'The negative interest rate acted as an encouragement for lenders to grant loans. For a short time, at least, lending in Sweden did appear to increase. However, it's unlikely that a low (or even negative) interest rate is enough on its own to stimulate a recovery.'

---

case study

Napoleon's holes – true or false?

An old economics teacher of mine would often repeat the following story.

After the retreat from Russia in 1812, Napoleon's army had shrunk to 100,000 demoralised and exhausted soldiers. There was little work for them back in France. So Napoleon made half of his ragged army dig holes. The other half filled them back in.

Why? Employed men pay taxes and they are not reliant on handouts from either the state or the church. Napoleon figured that work – even if it was meaningless – was better for morale than idleness. Given that he'd lost 500,000 men to famine, cold, exhaustion and the enemy, Napoleon probably felt he owed the survivors a favour.

True or false? I still don't know. But it's not the worst way to protect the economy from recession, is it?

I turned back to the flipchart. The thick line of lending moved up much quicker than the solid line. The growth in lending outpaced the increase in economic activity. I added a single word on the graph: *recovery.*

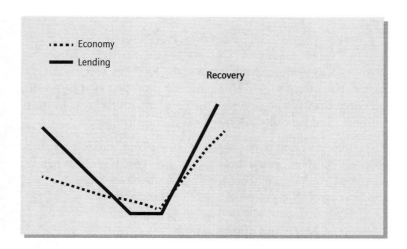

Day 4, 9.45am EST – APX Bank, New York

I glanced at the back of the room. Another latecomer, carrying a briefcase, sports bag and a gallon of coffee, fumbled in. He sat next to Karl, blocking his way out. Time now, I reckoned, for a training technique that's educationally very effective and would also give me valuable thinking time.

'I want you to form groups of four people. I want you to discuss what happens when the economy enters recovery. Time is tight, so I can only give you three minutes.'

I was out the door before Karl realised he was trapped in a group. I had a second to call Emily. I heard a rap on a window and saw Emily waiting for me in a breakout room. She beckoned me in.

'What's up?' I asked her.

'It's a disaster. Karl found your hotel room on my online credit card statement.'

'But ...'

'It looks bad.'

'No. It looks terrible.' Now I knew why Karl was looking daggers at me. But what sort of relationship did they have that he needed to check her bank accounts all the time? 'I'll take a break in thirty minutes and we can work out what to do with him.'

'No. I've just found out I've got an off-site today. I can't be contacted. Here, you'd better take my credit card. Whatever happens you're going to need money to move around.' Emily told me her PIN and I rushed back to the classroom.

What happens when the slump ends?

Breathlessly I asked the closest group, 'What happens to lending when consumer confidence turns from negative to positive?'

'People use credit cards and look for loans. Banks, who have taken a real beating during the slump because of bad debt, begin to lend. More mortgages are granted, more houses are bought and real estate agents start rubbing their hands together. Everyone is still cautious, but house prices will begin to move upwards.'

'Good answer. Next group. What is the impact of a rise in lending?'

'Employment will start to rise as companies look to expand. The amount of disposal income in the economy increases. People can rely on their salaries to be paid every month. Happiness spreads as people see that financial reins are loosened.'

I choose the group next to Karl's. 'How can a government spend its way out of a recession?'

'They can build new schools and upgrade hospitals. These infra-structure projects stimulate the economy. Builders have money, so there's less need for benefits. They'll spend their money in shops, so the High Street looks busier. Shop assistants – and shop owners – pay tax.'

'That's right. New jobs are created for baristas and people who invent names like *frappuccino*. Everything looks rosier and people sense they're in the recovery phase. But there's a big danger lurking on the horizon: *inflation*.'

Inflation rises when the recovery gets stronger

'Short-term inflation can be caused by increasing costs of production. When workers in a TV factory see beer costs more they demand more money. But their increased wages will put up the cost of TVs. A travel agent who wants a new TV will now also demand more pay. The increased cost of a holiday will be passed on to the TV assembler. Wages spiral upwards.

'Demand-pull inflation is caused when demand for products from individuals, companies and governments rises. We often see demand-pull inflation when we come out of a period of recession. A sudden excess of demand relative to supply means that prices go up. Natural disasters and war can also cause sudden shock inflation. The price of oil, which is essential for production and distribution, is especially susceptible to political events.

❝ Inflation doesn't hit everybody equally ❞

'Inflation doesn't hit everybody equally. If you're on a fixed income, you're going to take a bigger hit. The money a pensioner receives every month will be worth less because inflation destroys the value of money. By contrast, workers may be able to bargain for more money or move to another job.

'There's even one group of people who benefit from inflation. If you've got debts you actually get a gain from inflation because your repayments will be smaller than your debt. So, inflation is cruel because it harms people who've been prudent with their savings. High inflation makes it difficult for companies, governments and individuals to plan properly for the future. Budgets become useless because no one knows how much things will cost in the future.'

---

fast facts

Inflation is difficult to measure

Inflation is a rise in prices.

That's a simple enough statement but it's very hard to accurately measure how much prices have gone up. Governments use a basket of goods to measure price changes on the High Street but each country will choose different products. And the contents of the basket will change over time. We might include nicotine patches and exclude snuff, or measure the cost of apps but leave out DVDs. What, though, do we do with the cost of tattoo ink, tortilla wraps and online dating agencies?

In the short term, inflation is caused by imbalances between supply and demand of products and services in the economy. In the long term, it seems that the major cause of inflation is the money supply. Many economists feel that too much liquidity in the money markets (caused by easy lending, availability of credit and high levels of disposable income) will automatically turn a recovery into a boom.

There are three terms you need here. *Deflation* is a fall in price levels. *Hyper-inflation* occurs when inflation is out of control and money rapidly loses its value. *Stagflation* is the very dangerous combination of inflation, economic stagnation and high unemployment. It's a nightmare.

Day 4, 10.30am EST – APX Bank, New York

The interior designers at APX had obviously worked hard to erase any joy in the breakout area. Grey cups sat on dark blue tables, grey doors led into dark blue offices. A faded motivational poster – *None of us is as smart as the rest of us!* – hung on the laminated wood wall. Grey blinds blotted out a fantastic view of Manhattan.

Karl made a beeline for me as soon as break-time started. He was all smiles and shook my hand. But, in a voice too low for anyone else to overhear, he spoke to me through clenched teeth. 'You're in deep trouble, you idiot.'

'I can explain ...'

'I'm sure you can. But I'm not interested. You need to ...'

The Russian woman stood between us and introduced herself. Her name was Ksenia Something-Difficult. I smiled, grateful for the diversion, but Karl stormed away.

Happy days are here again

Day 4, 10.45am EST – APX Bank, New York

The audience was already waiting for me when I returned. 'Economies have short memories,' I began. 'People who were close to bankruptcy three years ago soon forget the troubles of the past when the economy heats up. Confidence increases when salaries increase. Richer people may look for a bigger house or may even consider a second home.

'Banks have to compete if they want to keep their share of the market. They offer big mortgages to people with small deposits. Clients they kicked out during the slump are welcomed back with open arms.'

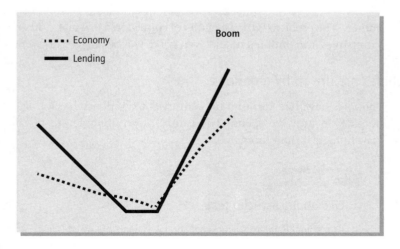

'In this phase of high growth, lending (the thick black line line) zooms away from the economy. Consumers pay more for goods so inflation rises. Unemployment vanishes and so salaries rise. Companies make more profits and take on more staff, paying extra to attract the right people.'

Boom time bubbles

A bubble occurs when market price parts company from fair value

'Any boom has the potential to turn into a bubble. Read any finance textbook and it will tell you – *a bubble occurs when the price of an asset is much higher than its intrinsic value.* This sort of explanation presupposes that there is a fair value for everything that can be bought and sold. A bubble occurs when the price rises well above this fundamental value.'

ff One thing we know about every bubble is that it will end in disaster 55

'One thing we know about every bubble is that it will end in disaster. The weakest companies will go bust first and the most indebted individuals soon collapse under the credit cards they've racked up. Investments in weak companies and in questionable sectors lose money. The problem is then a matter of contagion. How many other companies, bad, indifferent and even good, will be dragged down?'

Bubbles are driven by emotions

'Bubbles have been around for centuries. Confidence has a huge impact on how we spend. The causes of any bubble are more psychological than financial.'

case study

Lies about ostrich meat

At a school reunion several years ago I was unable to avoid Giles. He'd put all his hard-earned savings into ostrich eggs. He'd seen an advert which said the price of ostrich meat had grown by 30 per cent in each of the last two years. It was now £9 per kilo.

Why, he begged me, couldn't the price go up by 30 per cent per year forever?

Because, I told him, in twenty years, ostrich meat would cost £1,710 a kilo. Which is about twice the price of the world's finest truffles. In another decade, it would be more expensive than rhodium, the most expensive substance in the world.

Sadly, he thought my calculation was actually a strong reason to buy more ostrich eggs. Of course, his reasoning was ludicrous. If something's gone up very quickly, it's the most likely candidate to go down very quickly as well.

The fool in the herd

I then told the group that four possible psychological reasons explain why investment bubbles occur.

'The *greater fool theory* says that we all know that we're buying assets that are overvalued. It's just that we all believe that there's someone else who'll buy them from us. The world plays financial pass-the-parcel. When the music stops, the greatest fool of all is lumbered with the inflated asset.

'A second argument is *extrapolation*. This occurs when an investor looks at historical data and believes that those movements can continue into the future. *Herding* is another factor. It's a trait of human beings to move together. So fund managers who missed out on the early stages of a boom are often eager to buy in at a later stage. They over-pay for assets which are already inflated.'

I think my former classmate was guilty of all three of these traits. But he wasn't troubled by the fourth.

'*Moral hazard* is a phrase which the last great financial crisis introduced to us. It seemed that the governments of the world were willing to bail out certain financial institutions that were heading towards collapse. Directors of these companies benefited from huge potential upside whilst enjoying protection from the downside. Moral hazard skews the risk and return profile in favour of the risk taker. And this is sure to add to the bubble.'

case study

The truth about tulip mania

Newspaper articles often refer to tulip mania as the world's first financial bubble. But the truth is far less earth-shattering than you might have been led to believe.

The main culprit in the myth of tulip mania was Charles Mackay. He published a famous book – *Extraordinary Popular Delusions and the Madness of Crowds* – which painted seventeenth-century Holland as a hotbed of financial vice. A massive boom market in tulip bulb prices was blamed on a virus which produced fantastically colourful flowers which were very, very popular. Prices went through the roof. By 1636 a sort of futures market appeared where farmers could buy and sell bulbs.

The trade (if you can call it that) in tulip bulbs took place during a massive epidemic of bubonic plague. Many people buying and selling this particular commodity were sitting in pubs, drinking away their fears of imminent death. I like to see tulip mania as a fatalistic gambling game invented by drinkers who realised that money wasn't all that important.

Mackay, however, relied on contemporary sources which came from people who had a religious axe to grind. He tells the story of an immensely valuable tulip which was eaten by a sailor who mistook it for an onion. This story is very illustrative because it's obviously untrue. Tulips are poisonous and taste absolutely nothing like onions. (Don't try this at home. I've done the research for you.)

Tulip mania has become a byword for mass speculation and – more than anything else – financial stupidity. But relying on Mackay's account is akin to basing a history of twenty-first century ethics on clippings from *The News of the World*.

Day 4, 12.30pm EST – APX Bank, New York

Karl Honey had vanished from the room. I didn't know if that was good news or bad news.

I pointed to the top of our graph. 'What always happens when lending zooms so high above GDP?'

Mr Sleek answered. 'Complete freaking collapse!'

I laughed. 'Exactly right! Whatever we call it – the credit crunch, the banking crisis, or even the complete freaking collapse – it's inevitable.' I always use the abbreviation GFC to refer to the Global Financial Crisis of 2008. The excessive use of acronyms and abbreviations was one of Karl Honey's many irritating affectations. I started to worry more about his motives. But then I snapped back to the room and told them a little bit more about banking.

---

fast facts

A bit of law before we go any further

The Glass-Steagall Act was a piece of US legislation introduced after the Stock Market Crash of 1929. Glass-Steagall split banks into two groups: they could be a retail bank or an investment bank but not both.

The snappily-titled Gramm-Leach-Bliley Act of 1999 ended this distinction. Investment banks could now issue mortgages. Retail banks could now trade securities. The stage was set for a barnstorming decade in banking. What on earth could go wrong?

Well, for one thing, the Global Financial Crisis. The securitisation boom brought an investment banking frame of mind to a retail banking business. Instead of waiting patiently for home owners to ask for mortgages, bankers aggressively hunted for victims. But we run ahead of ourselves. We'll return to the GFC and securitisations later.

'The housing boom was encouraged by low interest rates globally. A glut of adverts promised low loan rates, but hid the details of the higher rates to come.

'A new phrase – *predatory lending* – entered the financial lexicon. Borrowers have always falsified their details to make their mortgage applications more appealing. But now lenders were also using fraud to process more mortgages. There are many stories of brokers hiding charges from their clients, or switching rates at the last minute.

'Successive interest rate rises in 2007 made it harder for borrowers to pay off their mortgages.'

'Why did the governments of the world put up interest rates?' Another good question from the woman in the black-framed spectacles.

❝ A crash is always brutally rapid ❞

'Because inflation was out of control. Wages were going up rapidly.' I turned back to the graph. 'A crash is always brutally rapid. A multitude of serious problems appear at the same time and confidence evaporates.

'The US property bubble ended with a tumble in house prices, an epidemic of foreclosures and a tidal wave of defaults. Contagion spread to other financial institutions and across country borders. Markets froze and governments found they couldn't borrow their way out of the hole. The GFC had arrived.'

Day 4, 6.00pm EST – APX Bank, New York

The afternoon of the course went well but I was happy to be heading back to London. The trip had provided me with more questions than answers. APX ordered me a cab to the airport. I've always loved that trip over the Brooklyn Bridge and was looking forward to some time to organise my thoughts.

But a grim-faced Karl Honey was waiting for me in the back.

'Are you following me, Karl? It seems that we are running into each other a lot these days.'

'Don't you believe in coincidences?'

'Not with this frequency.' The cab pulled off. 'What are you doing in my taxi?'

'You're meant to be the expert in the psychology of money. Why don't you take a guess? It would be interesting for me to see your powers in action for once. Emily has told me so much about your abilities, but it's always different in the flesh.'

It was forty-five minutes to the airport, more if the traffic was bad. I decided to humour him. 'Where do you want me to start?'

'Emily's told me about fear and greed. I think this would be a good time to learn more.'

So I told Karl about psychographics. 'We classify people by their personality and their wants. Even identical twins, brought up in exactly the same environment, will feel very differently about finance. We all have an emotional response to saving money and taking risks.'

'That all sounds very touchy-feely. Seems like a load of BS if you ask me.'

'Let me give you an example.' The traffic had ground to a halt.

'Imagine I offer you two bags. One has £50,000 and one has £100,000. I can give you the £50,000 now. Or you flip a coin.' The honking of angry horns on Tillary Street almost drowned out the second part of the deal. 'Heads you get the £100,000 bag. But tails gets you nothing. What do you take, and why?'

I could almost see the wheels spinning in Karl's head. Mathematically, both choices were worth £50,000. (The second offers 0.5 – a 50 per cent chance – of £100,000 and 0.5 of £0, which works out at £50,000.) But the first deal was guaranteed whilst the second deal was risky.

'I'm going to take the coin flip,' Karl said. 'But I want to add a refinement.'

'Go on.'

'If I get tails, I want £20,000. Think of it as downside protection.'

'Fine. Now the second choice is worth £60,000 (0.5 of £100,000 and 0.5 of £20,000). So you're after some more compensation for taking the risk, which is the rational thing to do. But think about the £20,000. You seem to be motivated by minimising your loss, rather than maximising your gain.'

'Whatever.'

'Let me try another deal and see if you bite.'

'Go on.'

'Tails still gets you nothing, but this time heads will pay £120,000. So it's also worth £60,000 (0.5 of £120,000 and 0.5 of £0). But can you see how it's different?'

'Sure. The player is motivated by more gain. They seem indifferent to the loss.'

'Correct.'

'So what?'

'People are different, Karl.' I couldn't help myself repeating one of Jerry Witts' favourite aphorisms. 'Money is the most sensitive nerve in the human body.'

He huffed and looked at his watch. 'Emily told me about all these stupid games you played on her grad course. But you're dealing with grown-ups now, so perhaps we can make it a bit more interesting.'

'What do you mean?'

'We could play for real money.'

'Very funny. I'm not the sort of man who customarily carries 120 grand on his travels.'

'But you are. In fact, you've carried about two million quid across the Atlantic Ocean.'

'What are you talking about?

'The train Uli bought you is worth two million pounds. Even more as prices go up.'

'It's worth about 180 Swiss francs. I checked at the toy shop when that guy handed it to me.'

'That guy? Oh, you mean Christof. He's been in on it since the beginning.'

'In on what, Karl? This isn't funny any more. I'm tired and I want to get back to London and live a normal life.'

'I don't think that will ever be possible.'

'Why the devil not?'

And then, of course I got it.

Rhodium. I've been lugging around two kilograms of rhodium in the shape of a stupid model train since I left the toy shop. Which meant that I've been a pawn in someone's plan since my meeting with Uli. Uli. Friendly, happy, not-particularly-bright Uli with his sudden bout of nerves and his mysterious new client. He couldn't have set this up, could he?

Karl said, 'We've been following your every move since you met Guy Abercrombie on the train from Zurich.'

'Who's *we*?'

'Us. The good guys.'

'What?'

'I'm investigating a massive fraud, but I'm not doing it for the media. That's my cover. My actual employers are more discreet and prefer to be low profile. This whole case could destroy the UK banking sector if it comes out.'

'How do I know you're telling the truth?'

'It's a risk you take. But I can prove it's not BS. You can check with a colleague of mine.'

'Who?'

'Anisa Chabbra.'

Great. Not only was Anisa also involved, but she'd been stringing me along since Zurich. I felt like the biggest fool the world had ever seen. I had to find out who else was involved in tricking me. 'What about Emily Prentice?'

'She's a nice girl, but she's just been part of my job. I think of her as something of a perk.' Karl grinned. 'There have been much worse ones.'

'That's heartless, Karl.'

'I know. But at least I won't get jealous about your hotel appearing on her credit card bill.'

'Listen, I can explain ...'

'No need. We need to get you somewhere safe before this all explodes. Take these tickets and you'll be met when you land.'

'But I don't need help to get across London.'

'No. But you might need a hand in Hong Kong.'

I stood on the sidewalk outside JFK with my single, small suitcase in my hand.

'TTFN,' Karl said, with the smirk of a winner on his face.

'You use a lot of abbreviations, Karl.'

'I know. Saves time.'

'But I don't know all of them.'

'I can translate.'

'Don't worry, I looked most of them up. I now know that GYAC is Give You A Clue.'

Karl stretched out his hand to say goodbye.

I smiled and turned towards him. 'There's also an alternative meaning.'

'Which is?'

'God You're A ...'

The roar of my missed London flight drowned me out.

Crash

Day 6, 4am HKT – Hong Kong

I arrived in Hong Kong in the dark. Some time during the night I'd lost a day of my life. I couldn't sleep. Jet-lag, stress and fear forced me to the minibar. Through the smog I made out the winking lights of Victoria Peak high above the overcrowded financial district. I turned the air-con up to max and headed for the shower.

Wide awake now, I read this review of how the housing bubble and the GFC were connected.

Homes fit for NINJAS

From Alabama to Washington, across the UK and continental Europe, then into Hong Kong and South Korea, the last housing bubble was absolutely massive. As early as 2004, economists were warning that housing was out of control. President Bush opined: 'If houses get too expensive, people will stop buying them.' With that sort of piercing insight, it's a wonder that Bush isn't held in higher regard.

The sources of the bubble are easy to find. It was a period of extremely low interest rates and massive over-confidence. The dot-com crash was a fading memory and the stock market was back to its booming best. Lending standards were relaxed. Even NINJAs – buyers with No Income, No Job and No Assets – were able to secure finance from eager banks. A new category of

❝ The sources of the bubble are easy to find ❞

mortgage holder was born: *sub-prime*. They were sold variable rate mortgages, with small or non-existent payments, and benefited from very low initial interest rates. When interest rates were put up – as they always are when an economy overheats – these were the borrowers who couldn't pay off their loans.

In March 2007, twenty-five sub-prime lenders had either declared bankruptcy, had publicly announced that they had massive losses on their properties and mortgage portfolio, or had put themselves up for sale. The European Central Bank and the US government pumped money into their economies, but it was too late. The total losses have been astronomical.

---

fast facts

Danger! CDO!

Retail banks traditionally made money by taking deposits and turning them into mortgages. Mortgages were moderately profitable and low risk, because the bank could always foreclose on the house if a problem occurred. But mortgages tied up the bank's capital for a long time.

The solution appeared to be CDOs: *collateralised debt obligations*. A CDO took a pool of mortgages – say half a billion pounds worth of lending – and turned them into bonds. The CDO broke the link between the bank and the mortgage holder. Now, it was the bond holders who would receive interest payments from the mortgages.

The retail bank sold the bonds to investors who wanted exposure to the mortgage market. The banks told their clients that CDOs were great investments which offered that elusive combination of high return and low risk.

Events took a weird turn when the banks started to believe their own publicity. If CDOs were such great investments, why didn't they buy some for themselves? In an amazing act of financial cannibalism, Bank A bought CDOs from Bank B and held them as investments. Bank B returned the favour by buying CDOs from Bank A.

The world's financial system began to feed off itself.

An envelope had been pushed under my door.

```
Be at the Man Mo Temple at 1pm. Walk, do not
take a cab.
```

The heat outside wrapped around me like a wet towel. In the steep streets of Western District I passed shops jammed with antique blackwood furniture, ceramic mah-jong tiles and terracotta statues of imperial warriors. In a corner of Hollywood Road I saw a small grouping of coffin shops, selling silk funeral clothes for the departed. Next to them was a stall selling counterfeit Rolexes.

From the hill I looked down at the shadows of the Bank of China Tower. The feng shui of the Tower is notorious. Many locals believe the building has been specially designed to send negative energy towards competitors. It is one of the ironies of modern-day finance that many banks create destructive vibes without any help from necromancers.

Credit risk

A bank buys and sells money. Or, to be a bit more exact than Mickey Rourke was in *Nine and a Half Weeks*, it's actually paying to rent money which it then lends out for a period of time.

A bank borrows money from retail customers and from other banks. The money the bank borrows is a liability. The borrowings are turned into customer loans, which produce income in the form of interest payments. Remember at this stage that a loan made by a bank to a customer is an asset for the bank.

The big risk is *credit risk*. This is the risk that the interest or, much worse, the principal which has been lent to a customer is not paid back. Shorter-term loans carry less risk because it's easier to predict defaults in the near future. Longer-term loans will always carry higher interest rates because there is more time for credit risk to appear.

Poor lending decisions will lead to bad debts. Impaired loans – those which have permanently fallen in value – create a hole in the asset side of a bank's balance sheet. If that hole isn't swiftly and decisively repaired, depositors will withdraw their money. A bank without depositors is like a shop without inventory. No one wants to stick around.

Born to run

During a banking crisis the value of a bank's assets plummets. It might be that their loans will not be repaid, or the bonds they've bought have been downgraded by the rating agencies, or their principal investments have gone bust. Often it's all of these events at exactly the same time.

A run on the bank happens when depositors realise these disasters. They'll rush to Bank A to withdraw their savings. Media images of people queuing up outside Bank A, smoking nervously and looking harried, appear on our screens. The queue outside Bank A is replicated at Banks B, C and D.

Bank E is now incredibly reluctant to lend to anyone else because the risks are too high. In this way banks actually accelerate the impact of the banking crisis. You now see contagion. People shun even safe banks because the system is rotten. No one wants to entrust their money to a bank that might go bust the next day.

---

case study

Dick the Gorilla

Dick Fuld was CEO during the collapse of Lehman Brothers. Even his nickname – 'the Gorilla of Wall Street' – was rubbish.

Money came easily to Lehman Brothers in the boom years after the dot-com crash. Profit after tax was $4.2 billion in 2007, compared to $113 million thirteen years earlier. Big profits came from CDOs. Proprietary trading was relatively easy when the prices of all assets were booming. Indeed, Fuld expressed his distaste for mid-decade pessimists in characteristically colourful language: 'When I find a short-seller, I want to tear his heart out and eat it before his eyes while he's still alive.'

Fuld's bullying leadership style pushed the firm forward but meant that he was surrounded by yes-men. His judgements were rarely challenged by directors who were either too loyal or too frightened to ask the difficult questions. He made them all rich, which helped, but not as rich as he made himself. Analysis of the notes to Lehman's accounts show that Fuld earned $300 million in the eight years before the bank's crash.

Lehman's stock price dropped 48 per cent in a single trading session. Yet Fuld still believed he was right. Like a silly Canute, Fuld tried to hold back the market. He believed that the US government would not lose face and allow a major financial institution to fail. But contagion spread. The bank's lenders refused to stump up more cash and creditors clamoured for payment. No one would trade with Lehman because of the risk of non-payment. Fuld and his firm found themselves at the centre of the death spiral.

Lehman filed for bankruptcy protection on 15 September 2008. It had 26,000 staff and a brand established over 158 years of banking. Fuld had presided over the biggest corporate disaster in history. Under his hubristic leadership, a business with a market cap of $42 billion was worth precisely nothing.

Day 6, 1.00pm HKT – Hong Kong

I watched the people scurrying into the Man Mo Temple and rushing out, two minutes later, with the same worried look on their faces. Even prayer was fast in HK. Inside the cavernous temple incense coils filled the darkness with clouds of white smoke. I stood next to a tiny, grey-haired Chinese man dressed in a black business suit who held a caged bird in his hand.

He turned towards me and, without prompting, told me, 'Both the police and the gangsters worship the same deity here. They stand side by side, paying their respects, and then they go out and fight against each other.'

We walked outside together. He led me to a ledge over the Kowloon Straits and pointed to the Star Ferry building and the new developments in Tsim Sha Tsui. 'The water in the Straits used to be smooth like glass. My grandfather told me that a thin woman could walk across it in ten minutes.'

He ran a claw-like hand through his thick grey hair. 'Every year we move the river banks nearer to each other. So now the water is choppy when you take the Star Ferry, and you cannot read a newspaper on the deck because of the waves. So many boats and ships, so many wakes competing with the tide. The Straits are like Hong Kong. Like the whole of Asia and the whole of the globe. People are always trying to force more beer into a smaller bottle. Something has to give.'

I wiped sweat from my brow.

'Isn't there a saying you English have?'

'What?'

'You need a long spoon to sup with the devil. I would like you to meet my boss.'

Back inside the temple some of the smoke had cleared. I half-recognised a bulky form sitting on a chair at the front of the room.

I was surprised, I guess, but not shocked.

My appointment was with Mr Conrad, the mysterious investor from the Zurich to Paris express.

23

Scam

Day 6, 2.00pm HKT – Restaurant, Hong Kong

El Diablo, at the top of a forty-two-storey tower, displayed no menus in its smoked glass windows. In my experience this was always a forewarning of outrageous pricing, as was the liveried doorman who greeted us. Still, I rather suspected that Conrad had the money to pay the bill.

'Have a glass of this wonderful Sancerre and I'll tell you why I've invited you here.'

I felt under-dressed and under-prepared. 'I think I know.'

'I doubt that, my old friend.' But Conrad's smile and easy charm vanished. 'What do you know about Cal-Pan?'

'A lot. But I want something in return if I help you.'

'What?'

'Complete protection from legal cases. Immunity from arrest. My career continues without incident.'

'That's quite a list.'

'And there's quite a lot of money at stake with Cal-Pan.'

Conrad forced out a smile but his eyes stayed cold. Why was he so focused on Cal-Pan? I had thought that Guy Abercrombie was to be the subject under discussion.

'Can I remind you that I'm not the one who is this far' – Conrad tensed his finger a millimetre away from his thumb – 'from the collapse of his glorious career. I can leak your involvement with Cal-Pan to the press. Your comfortable life will be over.'

I stared at the scrunched-up frown lines on Conrad's forehead. They formed a mark like a cloven foot. 'OK,' I finally said. 'I promise to return with some more information by breakfast time.'

'Promises are dangerous. A wise man once told me that if you buy a pig on credit you'll always hear it grunting.'

The exhaustion of the day hit me hard. 'Who was the wise man?'

'Jerry Witts.'

Another part of the puzzle was to be revealed.

The truth about rhodium

I ran out of El Diablo and headed back to the Mandarin. I didn't care what time it was or who was listening in to my phone.

'What's Cal-Pan, Emily?'

'It's a company that doesn't exist. We invented it.' The line was surprisingly clear but I couldn't believe my ears.

'What on earth are you talking about?'

'Cal-Pan was so we could trick them, not you. The more Conrad and his cronies looked at it, the less they would see what we were up to. Uli hid a copy of the report in your briefcase to see whether it passed muster. We never thought for a second you'd fall for it too.'

'Fall for what?'

'A completely fake company. It doesn't exist. We made up the research. I fed Karl the disinformation and he reported back to his paymasters. They were so blinded by greed they missed what was right in front of them.'

'How does Karl fit into all of this? I thought you were in love with him.'

'He's not my type. Come on, you know me better than that.

The last film he saw was *The Bonfire of the Vanities*. He absolutely adored it, the idiot!'

'So there was never anything between you two?'

'I saw him coming from a mile away. I've been feeding him false info since our first kiss. And doctoring photos. I Photoshopped a picture of your face on to Uli's body. He was in the pub with Guy five years ago, not you. I owe you a big apology for that.'

'Why did you …?'

Emily pre-empted my question. 'Because I want them to look stupid.'

'But Emily, you're taking a massive risk. These people are policing for the financial markets. They are the eyes and ears of the world's governments.'

'No they're not. They're conmen.'

'What?'

'Conrad is the crook who ripped off my parents. And Karl Honey has been his little lapdog for years. Karl's lazy and he doesn't check his stories. We'll keep making up tales about the new supply of rhodium so the price plummets. And then we'll tell him the spent nuclear fuel rods will be contaminated for hundreds of years.

'Why?'

'I've sold the world's first rhodium call option. It's got a life of nine months. The premium of $12 million has already been paid to APX. I want the price of rhodium to zoom upwards so the counterparty makes a fortune.'

'What happens to APX? They'll be furious.'

'They'll hush it all up. They certainly don't want to lose their reputation over a high-profile deal like this. And then I'll go for the kill.'

I heard footsteps in the corridor. They stopped outside my room. I dropped my voice to a whisper. 'What?'

> **❝ If investors don't trust a market they will pull out ❞**

'I'll leak the story of the market manipulation and the cover-up to the press. If investors don't trust a market they will pull out. No one will trade rhodium. And I will have saved a tiny part of the world from exploitation.'

---

case study

How to manipulate a market

The Flaming Ferraris were a group of image-conscious traders at CSFB (Credit Suisse First Boston).

The FFs took a large short position in the Swedish Stock Exchange index. (A stock market index is the best indicator of how well the stock market of a country is performing.) They hoped the index would close down on the last day of the year, guaranteeing themselves bonuses for the year.

A junior trader manipulated the index downwards by aggressive selling of Enso Stora, the largest paper and pulp company in the world. The index of a small country is always dominated by a few companies. The whole index is moved by a change in the price of a company with a large market cap. The traders knew that Enso Stora was a big component of the index. If Enso Stora fell, the index would tumble.

The man behind the trades was James Archer, son of the disgraced British peer and perjurer, Jeffrey. Archer junior used a mobile phone, in direct contravention of trading rules, to place his trades. Stora's share price plunged from 90 kroner to 60 kroner in minutes. And the index had to follow suit. He put his plot into action on the quiet days between Boxing Day and New Year's Eve. But the fraud was easily spotted and the inevitable bans, fines and sackings followed.

Dressed like a posh version of the criminals from *Reservoir Dogs*, the FFs were named after a rum-based cocktail which is set on fire

> and drunk through a straw. Flaming Ferraris leave a disgusting
> aftertaste and make you look like an idiot. The drink is no better.
> Boom, boom.

I put the phone down. Whoever was waiting outside had stopped moving. Was this the moment when everything went wrong?

It would be easy for me to gloss over the events which had led me to this hotel room. I would love to present myself as the hero of the hour but I was simply a jet-lagged, twitchy man with no idea what to do next. I believe, deep down, that I'm a good man. I've always tried to see both sides of any argument. I'm a good listener, which is not something you can say about most presenters. I may come across as cocky (or even arrogant) when you first meet me, but that's normal in any attention-seeking profession like teaching.

From the moment I caught that Zurich train my life had been controlled by others. On one side there were Conrad, Karl Honey and Anisa. On the other side was Emily. I thought I knew her, but she was much changed from the naive young grad I had taught so many years before. She had invented a company and now she was planning to wreck a market. And how was Guy Abercrombie connected to this mess?

There was a knock on the door. Was it better to choose the devil I already knew?

Another knock. Paralysed with fear, I did nothing.

A third knock. I got up to face my fate.

It was Emily Prentice.

'How the devil did you ...'

'Simple. Karl used the internet at the bank to buy your flight tickets. I've read all his emails since he came to New York. He uses the same password on every account.'

'What is it?'

'His initials, of course. KEH. The E is for Ernesto, which was a surprise when I saw his birth certificate.'

'Which was...?'

'Saved as a scan on his desktop. I could steal his whole identity, if it were worth anything.'

'When did you ...?'

'About six hours before you. I was lying about the off-site in New York. They've no idea I'm here. I've been in Hong Kong for twelve hours now. You're using one of my credit cards so it was very easy to find out where you're staying.'

'Is there anything else you've been lying about, Emily?'

'Yes. No.' Emily paused. 'Maybe I need something cool from Room Service before I start with the explanation.'

Teamwork in action

But before she began, back in her room, I told her about Conrad and his interest in Cal-Pan.

Emily thought for a moment and decided on our next step. 'I want you to stay quiet. He obviously doesn't know that it's a fake story. We have to use his lack of knowledge to our advantage.'

'What about rhodium? Is that all a figment of your imagination as well?'

'No. It's all true. We're going to corner the market. Rhodium is only traded in London and three places in Switzerland.

'Zurich?'

'Yes.'

'Is Uli's fund helping you do the trade?'

'Yes.'

'Uli's been in on this since the beginning, hasn't he?'

She nodded. 'When did you realise?'

'I had an inkling in New York. When you told me about your parents you let slip you'd spoken to him.'

'Silly mistake.' She giggled, and bubbles of Cuba Libre appeared at the end of her straw.

'Apart from Uli, who else is in on the plot?'

Emily's face turned serious. This was going to be the moment of truth.

'All of us.'

'All of us?'

'The Goodman Rozel cohort. Your graduates.'

'What on earth are you talking about?'

'Teamwork. Being the best you can be. Looking for opportunities. All those things you taught us.'

'I don't understand.'

'It's us. You turned a collection of strangers into a group of friends. We're more than still in touch. We've been working together for years.'

'Please explain.'

'Look at the picture that Anisa sent through to you. Now fast forward ten years. What are all these people doing?'

I flicked it up on my screen. 'I don't know. Tell me.'

'Uli trades more or less everything in Zurich, right? He can put through the rhodium trade with no one batting an eyelid. Billy Blatt, as you know, is an expert in derivatives. Sergei the Russian has great access to capital.'

'So they can do the trade, no problem. I see that. But how on earth can you be so sure the price of rhodium will fall?'

'Do you see her? The clever girl who studied English? That's Ella Holroyd, who now writes market reports for various well-read financial websites. And him? Guillaume Mussot, who's risen to junior partner at a financial PR giant. And that's Tony Chew, who will be presenting the business news on this country's biggest TV channel in, oh, three minutes.'

'You're mad. You'll all get caught.'

'Look again. Eve Williams has worked in regulation for the last decade and knows every trick in the book. Oliver Green went on to study corporate law and is now king of the loophole. Sissoun Ward works for the Director of Public Prosecutions. She's very well placed when it comes to losing important files.'

I scanned the faces again. 'Who's this one?'

'Bella Fleming. Her family own a chain of foreign exchange offices.'

Of course, I thought. How absolutely perfect for money laundering.

'This guy?'

'Richard Rouse. Runs the middle office of APX in Singapore. Next to him is Chris Baker, who's in charge of the back office.'

'Where?'

'In Singapore, naturally. We've pretty much thought of everything.'

'What about her?'

'Ffion Wilcox is the lead partner at APX's auditors. Isiah Bashkina, to her right, runs the finance department at APX.'

'This one?'

'Jake Waters. He's a financial whizzkid who now lives in a small castle near Berwick. His computer models helped us time the trade to perfection.'

There were still four people Emily hadn't included. 'What about Caroline Levy?'

'Runs an offshore hedge fund.'

'Augusto Astudillo?'

'Finance director at a commodity broking firm.'

'Winston Gadd?'

'Career criminal, I'm afraid. He's been useful.'

Guy was in the centre of the picture, next to me. Which meant there was one student left without a role in the conspiracy. One square peg that never fitted in.

'Don't tell me Robin Bearfield is involved in this as well.'

'No,' Emily said in a voice that dropped to a whisper. 'Robin was always a bit of a problem, wasn't he?'

No, I thought. No, no, no. Robin would not have joined in. He was the blackest of black sheep. And she was talking about him in the past tense. I know what people are capable of when fear and greed collide. The worst possible scenarios filled my mind.

'Emily?'

'Yes.'

'I need a straight answer to a straight question.'

'Yes.'

'Where's Robin Bearfield?'

---

case study

The value of a good contacts book

Hedge fund owner Raj Rajaratnam was a well-connected man. He was the kingpin in a massive share fraud which relied on associates who were handily placed in other firms. The Sri-Lankan-born billionaire made $63.8 million by buying insider information for his hedge fund, Galleon. The fund was focused on investments in the hi-tech sector, where the value of shares can rise massively on the news of a takeover bid.

Rajaratnam has maintained his innocence, despite wiretaps which the prosecutors used to prove his activities. These techniques – familiar to all of us who love *The Sopranos* – recorded Rajaratnam talking to senior executives across the business world. Former schoolmates and an employee at the ratings agency Moody's told him about upcoming takeovers. One Galleon employee got advance financial results from her boyfriend, a senior exec at IBM.

At least nineteen of Rajaratnam's contacts have pleaded guilty to leaking tip-offs in exchange for illegal payments. Some of them were lifelong friends who worked in senior positions at the consultancy McKinsey.

What's astonishing about Rajaratnam is the systematic way in which he persuaded Wall Street insiders to help him. He certainly wasn't a man who stumbled across sensitive information by accident. This was a professional who claimed he wasn't clear on the line between 'permissible detective work' and 'insider trading'. The difference is very easy to see: the first is legal and the second gets you eleven years in prison.

Weird fact – Robert Khuzami, director of enforcement at the Securities and Exchange Commission (SEC), suggested that the super-wealthy Rajaratnam was motivated by a need for social validation rather than greed. 'He's not a master of the universe, but rather a master of the Rolodex,' said Khuzami in a neat phrase which, incidentally, suggests that the SEC is not on the cutting edge of technology.

Emily didn't tell me about Robin Bearfield's whereabouts. Instead, she rested her head on the pillow and spoke softly to me. 'Do you want to know the plan?'

'Go on.'

'We're just about to discredit all our rumours about new sources of rhodium. The world will know there's no new mine in China and no secret strategic reserve held at Fort Knox. When the market realises supply is less than expected, the price of rhodium will rocket.'

'What about that story you told me about spent nuclear fuel being a possible source of rhodium. Was that a lie as well?'

'Not strictly, no. But it will take years for that to happen. I wanted to practise the story before I told it to Karl. I think he's hawking the story around the world's newspapers even as we speak. The more people he tells, the better for us.'

'What happens next?'

'All the stories are denied or proved false. The price goes up and ...'

'And?'

'The holder of the call option makes a fortune. APX has to pay them because it's a zero sum game.'

'Money. So that's what this is all about.'

Emily blushed. 'Not just money. I also want to save more countries from rape, murder, child labour, slavery and corruption. I think that's quite a laudable aim.'

'But you will make money if this works, won't you?'

'Sure, but money isn't the be all and end all. I only want enough to cover the losses my parents have suffered. And I'd be quite happy if I managed to bankrupt the shysters who've ripped them off. But if there's one thing I've learned since your course, it's that money can't buy happiness and it just tends to make misery more miserable.'

'But you still make millions of dollars. What will you do with the profits?'

'Give them to Guy, of course.'

'Why?'

'So he can give them away.'

'What?'

'I'll have to explain about Guy later.'

'Can I say that I think you're crazy and it will never work?'

'It's worked already. The counterparty is already up on the deal.'

I was flabbergasted. 'Who on earth is the counterparty?'

'This person here. I've got a feeling you might have heard of him.'

She took a dainty sip of her cocktail and handed me a contract note. I know I shouldn't have been surprised by the name, but to be honest I was shaking. It was, of course, Jerry Witts.

Not now, I prayed, please don't get in touch, Jerry. The last thing I needed was my former boss to reappear and demand the third favour.

'Are you OK?' Emily asked. 'You seem to have started daydreaming.'

'I'm fine. How is Jerry these days?'

'Jerry died two years ago from cirrhosis of the liver.'

'But you've told me he was your counterparty for the rhodium option.'

'No one at APX noticed he'd died because they were too busy thinking about the next commission. His wife kept his trading account open. She'd email orders every few months to make it look like Jerry was still alive. In fact, in one year the dead man was one of our most successful clients.'

I stopped for a second. 'What's Jerry's wife called?'

'Perrine. Perrine Witts. She's very nice. Have you ever met her?'

24

Revelations

Day 6, 7.00pm HKT – Emily's hotel room, Hong Kong

Is there a master plan?

We sat on Emily's bed and she ordered champagne. She sipped slowly as she told me the sad story of Guy Abercrombie.

'It started when Guy was asked by his other directors to test the bank's new security systems. They had suspicions about a clerk in the back office and wanted to test whether she could siphon off money. They gave Guy access to client accounts, security codes and all the passwords he could ever need. One Saturday morning he went into the office. Within ten minutes he sent some money from one client's secret account to an anonymous account in the Bahamas. Ten minutes later the money was wired back into the original account. No one was any the wiser.'

Guy told the directors that the system was flawless. 'The truth was that an eight-year-old could break the system. Guy treated it as a game, a harmless pastime to get him through another boring day in the office. Then he started to steal small amounts. The interest on the interest was how he phrased it.'

'Why?'

'There was never any great master-plan. Guy just went a bit mad, that's all. It's the money, you see. He saw so much of it, and all in the wrong hands. All those terrible crimes that had been committed by people who escaped justice. Guy's disappearance wasn't part of the plot. Poor lamb.'

'You told me earlier that Guy will get the surplus money from your rhodium options. And then you told me that he would just give it away. What did you mean by that?'

'Guy believed he was returning the money to its rightful owners. He became disgusted with what he saw in banking. The people he stole from were the worst of the worst. Currency traders who'd bankrupted entire countries. Bankers who'd paid themselves a fortune and then begged the government to bail them out. Corrupt presidents who stole aid money.'

I thought back to those Zurich cellars. I had walked over looted money and my conscience didn't blanch. My greed had blinded me to the misery contained in those vaults of gold.

Emily continued. 'Wherever Guy travelled he saw the homeless and the ill sleeping rough outside banks. I doubt whether Guy knew he had a conscience, but he knew that the financial markets were morally wrong. The inequality made him crack. He wanted to give £1 million away to the poor. That was loose change to Guy's clients. But it would buy fifty dialysis machines for kidney patients in Cambodia.'

'So what did he do?'

'He took £10,000 from 100 different clients. He went to his own bank and drew the amounts out as cash over a period of months. He went on holiday to Cambodia and left a suitcase stuffed with cash in a Buddhist temple. He figured they weren't likely to keep the money!'

'But what Guy did was wrong. You might think Guy is some sort of modern Robin Hood but the police regard him as a thief. There's still a huge amount of money that hasn't been traced.'

'True. Guy told his co-directors they needed to dispose of old statements and client records to cover their backs in the event of a raid by the financial authorities. It had to be done over the weekend in conditions of absolute secrecy. Guy volunteered to organise the work while the other directors went skiing. He stole millions and millions in cash.'

'A million dollars in $100 bills weighs 10 kilograms. He'd need a lorry to steal that much cash.'

'Or a rubbish truck. Guy was inspired by your little tale of the shredded dollars in the back of the dustbin lorry. He bought a second-hand rubbish truck from the council in Strasbourg. They had to sell it off, you see, because of the austerity cuts.'

Emily told me that the helpful removal men hired by APX filled the lorry up with bin bags stuffed full of banknotes. 'No one looks twice at a rubbish truck trundling along a motorway,' she said. 'And no one can read the number plates because they're covered with filth.'

'Why didn't he steal gold?'

'Far too heavy. And he wants the money to fly!'

---

case study

Rogue traders of the world unite and take over

As we near the end of this book, it might be good to remind ourselves of the perils of not learning.

Nick Leeson's destruction of Barings provides us with a perfect case study of how one determined person can lose a billion. Sixteen years later, Kweku Adoboli managed to more than double Leeson's high score whilst working for UBS. The Swiss banking giant had just managed to scrape through the GFC with significant help from its government. Yet now they had lost over $2 billion through poor internal controls.

Adoboli, like Leeson before him, was a back-room boy who became a derivatives trader. He was able to hide his massive losses because he knew exactly how to falsify records. For three years he got away with it, despite posting the cry for help *I need a miracle* on his Facebook profile. As with Barings, a failure to properly control traders was central to the unauthorised trading.

The response from top management at UBS was heavy on the jargon. The bank would adopt a more *client- centric strategy* and

> acknowledge the *new paradigm* in the financial markets. This latest disaster increased the clamour for retail banks to split away from 'casino' businesses such as hedge funds and proprietary trading.
>
> **Weird coincidence** – Adoboli was represented in court by Kingsley Napley. This is the law firm which advised Nick Leeson all those years ago.

When Emily told me of Guy's plan I burst out laughing. It was simple and funny and absolutely crazed.

'He's driving the truck around Europe, even as we speak. I think the first stop is the Acropolis. He wants to open a few bags and watch the money floating under the Athenian stars. Those people could do with a bit of joy and happiness for once. Then he plans to visit Warsaw, Lisbon, Madrid and even Dublin. All the places that have been destroyed by the crisis. Eventually he'll cross from Tarifa into Morocco and keep going into Africa until the money runs out.'

'This is absolutely mad. You do realise that Guy's picture is going to be all over the press?'

'So what?' Emily snapped back. 'Who cares? We've done something good with this money for a change, and all you can think about is the media.' She handed me a glass of champagne. 'Now can you drink this and shut up!'

I figured I could. We sat in silence for a couple of minutes before I asked her, 'What's the next move?'

'I've already booked you on a plane back to London tomorrow morning. It's probably safer if you stay here tonight rather than going back to your hotel.'

'What are you going to do?'

'I need to get out of Hong Kong as well. I'm going to help Guy, so I can't really tell you where I'm heading. I guess my story ends here.'

'There's just one more thing. Why have I been carrying the train around?'

'Later,' she said. 'You'll find out later.'

---

case study

Downfall

Every crisis needs a focus for our anger. Sometimes we have to search hard for someone to blame. But, occasionally, central casting sends us the perfect pantomime villain. Step forward, Fred the Shred, the curtains are opening.

Sir Fred Goodwin turned the low-profile Royal Bank of Scotland (RBS) into his own personal fiefdom. During his nine-year reign of fear Goodwin acquired upwards of twenty-five other financial institutions. Even his best friends would not describe this as a successful strategy. RBS collapsed and had to be propped up with an eye-watering £20 billion of taxpayers' money.

Goodwin pushed for the acquisition of a major chunk of ABN Amro in 2007, against the advice of many who warned that he was buying at the very top of the market.

People didn't like the fact that Goodwin was entitled to a pension of £703,000. And they didn't like Goodwin's justifications for taking the money. It was a contractually agreed amount, he opined, and there was no way he could forgo it. This was an egregious example of moral hazard. After years of taking risk and making money, Goodwin was rewarded for taking risk and losing money. Goodwin offered no apology.

When I woke up Emily had already gone. She'd left me a pre-printed boarding pass for a flight back to London. It was economy class and no hold luggage was allowed. I should have seen it as a bad omen, but I was too tired to read the signs.

I slept all the way to London, slept by the baggage carousel and slept in the taxi back to my home. The police were waiting for me at my house in Marylebone with a list of questions as long as your arm. I asked them for half an hour to unpack, shower and change. They gave me fifteen minutes. My hair was still wet as I took my place in the back of their car.

The teacher/student relationship

Day 8, 10.00am GMT – Whitehall, London

Some people don't change with time. They just get worse.

Stomach tensed with fear, I waited outside the office flanked by the two officers. There was no chair, and I tried my best not to look like a naughty schoolboy called in to see the headmaster.

'We meet again.' The first rays of a weak sun silhouetted his spindly frame.

'Yes, indeed we do.'

'How long has it been since our paths last crossed?'

'Eight years? Nine?'

'Eleven. You should be more accurate, especially when numbers are concerned.' Arms crossed tightly across his pigeon chest, Robin Bearfield emitted a little self-satisfied chuckle as he began his questions. 'You seem to have been busy. Especially in the last week. I do hope you're collecting air miles.'

Even Robin's jokes had got worse. But there was nothing I could do but smile and pretend he was funny.

Robin Bearfield clicked his tongue and the tutting sound echoed around his office. 'You really should have stayed in this country. All that flying around and avoiding Anisa makes you look guilty. As do those furtive meetings in hotel rooms and using another person's credit card.' He pointed to a chair and ordered me to sit. 'Now tell me about the train.'

'The train?'

'Yes.'

Robin Bearfield, rising star of the European Fraud Investigation Committee, could have asked me about Conrad or Emily or Karl or Guy Abercrombie. Instead, all he wanted to know about was the train.

'Where is it?'

'I left it at Hong Kong airport. I couldn't take it on the plane. I threw it away with a half-empty bottle of water just before customs.'

'I see. Do you have any idea why the train was so important?'

'No,' I lied.

'Or what is was worth?'

'No.' I always find it easy to keep lying once I've decided to be dishonest. 'I have absolutely no idea what you're talking about.'

'Emily wanted you to be arrested on the train from Zurich. She wanted to distract the police so that Guy could leave the train. So she gave you something to alert every customs officer from here to Timbuktu. The train was stuffed with a precious metal called rhodium.'

I shook my head and added another lie to my collection. 'Never heard of it.'

'It's very specialised. I'm absolutely flabbergasted that you didn't get caught at Zurich, or Paris, or New York.'

'How did he get off?'

'Again it was nothing complicated. He left at Strasbourg. Anisa thought he was with you in the dining car. You thought he was with his passengers in his carriage. He left his case and clothes and stepped off the train. We found him on the surveillance tapes. He was dressed as a dustman.'

Robin pressed a button on his phone. 'Yes. I ordered tea and biscuits twenty minutes ago. Where the devil are they?' He drummed the fingers of his right hand on the table. Strasbourg, I thought to myself. That's where Guy had parked the rubbish truck.

'When Abercrombie didn't come back from lunch with you, Anisa panicked. That's why we stopped the train at Nancy. We've been following Guy for days following a tip-off from his bank. An auditor rang them to say that money had disappeared from a client's account. Apparently her husband had died and she was having the contents of his will audited.'

'Can you tell me her name?'

'I don't see any harm in that. Her name was Perrine Witts.'

A knock on the door announced the arrival of Bearfield's precious sugar rush. Bearfield jumped towards the trolley and, without offering the plate to me, grabbed a handful of Jaffa Cakes. The trolley only carried one cup and one saucer.

'How does Conrad fit in with this?' I asked.

'He's a fraudster. He travels the world hoping to drum up cash from fools who don't know any better.'

'Don't tell me it was a coincidence that Conrad was on the train. What was he doing there?'

'Anisa Chabbra was secretly working for him. He'd blackmailed her. He was going to reveal that she'd bought all her qualifications. She didn't want to lose her job so she became his eyes and ears in my department. He paid her a fortune as well. She seemed to have developed quite a taste for designer labels since meeting Mr Conrad.'

Bearfield stirred four heaped teaspoons of sugar into his cup. 'We taped her calls, you see. It was actually quite hurtful to hear Anisa call Conrad *her boss*. Still, she won't be working here for much longer. After I've dealt with you, she'll be arrested as well.'

'As well?'

'Yes. As well as you. It was sheer bad luck that you got involved in all of this. But I don't think you can go home right away. I want you to tell me everything you learned about Emily Prentice and Guy Abercrombie. I need to find them.'

'What happens if I don't help you?'

'Perjury. Obstructing the police with their enquiries. Maybe fraud and racketeering if we can find some more evidence.' Bearfield stood up jerkily and fired out his last question. 'What's it to be?'

How it all ended

I assumed Guy Abercrombie's fraud would be a massive story. But it barely caused a ripple in the press and there was no mention of it on TV. A couple of blogs tried to spread rumours of a conspiracy involving Freemasons. But for most people it was obviously business as usual. Plenty of other bankers have disappeared recently, and who would shed a tear for yet one more?

I can only watch one hour of television a day. So I've sadly given up on movies, and instead I watch the news. No one has yet filmed Guy in the act of opening one of his rubbish bags, but his impact has been well documented. The police have had no luck in tracking him down and a huge crowd of cheering people chasing money is an effective smokescreen.

The press call them *flash mobs*, but that's so last year. On Facebook – where Guy has a certain notoriety – his many friends call them *money storms*. When I first watched the crowds running around London Bridge I thought they were rioters. But people were laughing and smiling, not looting and burning. The cash fluttered down from the Shard and I understood that all Guy Abercrombie wanted to do was spread some happiness.

Can you believe Guy called me after his last money storm?

The line crackled and buzzed like all payphones do. His voice was calmer than I had imagined. I heard neither shame nor pride, but his tone suggested satisfaction with a job well done.

'You should write a book about everything that happened,' Guy half-joked.

I told him I'd already had that idea. 'There's no hurry. I've got plenty of time to finish it.'

I heard lorries thundering past, the sound of a motorway service station anywhere in the world. He said goodbye and put down the phone, and I wondered if I'd ever hear from my ex-student again.

My work once took me around the world. But I won't see Wall Street or Shanghai or Cairo for at least another year. I used to love talking in front of people but there's not much of an audience these days. The penny dropped but it was me who had to do the learning.

That chance meeting with Guy Abercrombie changed my life forever. My problems began on that damn Zurich train. I thought I knew about secret techniques and cunning schemes but I was gravely mistaken. While writing this book I've continually asked myself this question: why me?

I had one of the great jobs. Now all I have is a toy train stashed under some microwavable pizzas at the bottom of my freezer. I don't know how much is waiting for me until I get out of prison, but that's risk and return in action.

Index